KT-145-824

$\mathcal{P}$RINT STYLE

*

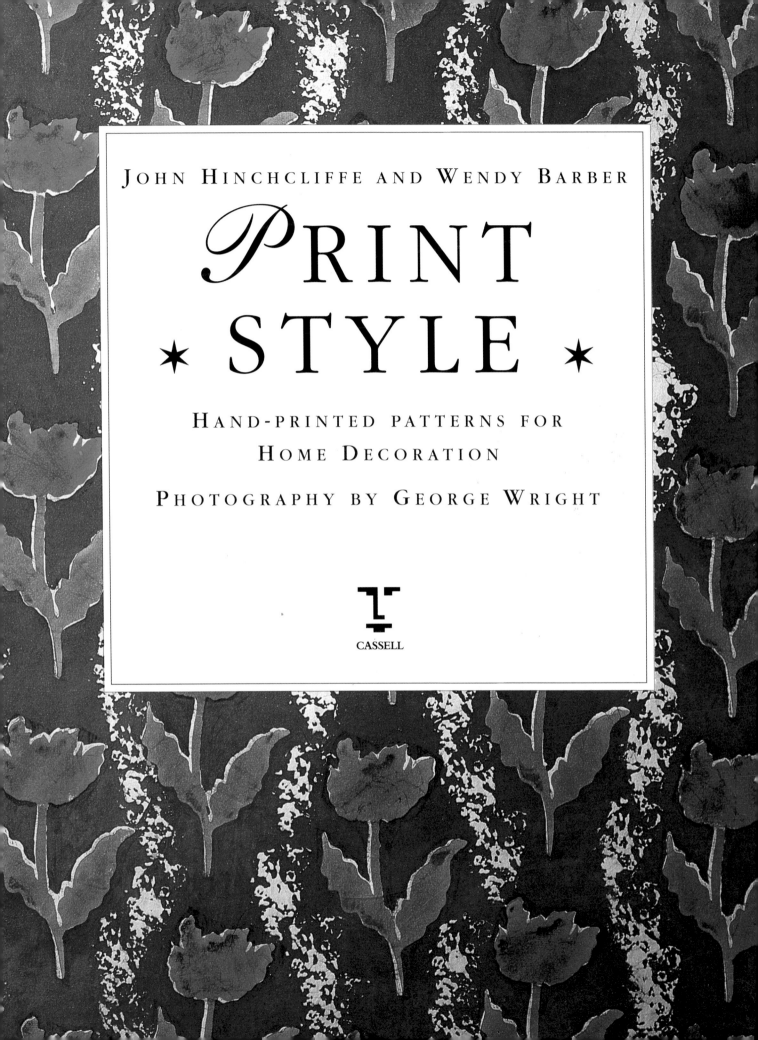

JOHN HINCHCLIFFE AND WENDY BARBER

PRINT STYLE

★ ★

HAND-PRINTED PATTERNS FOR
HOME DECORATION

PHOTOGRAPHY BY GEORGE WRIGHT

CASSELL

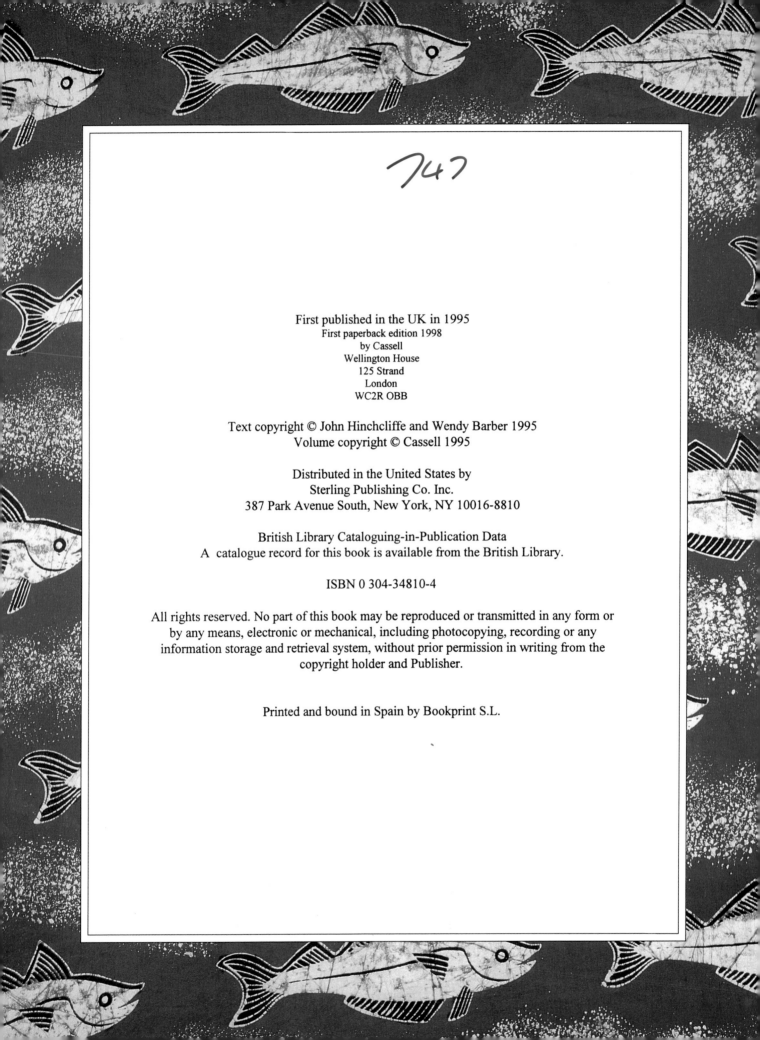

747

First published in the UK in 1995
First paperback edition 1998
by Cassell
Wellington House
125 Strand
London
WC2R OBB

Text copyright © John Hinchcliffe and Wendy Barber 1995
Volume copyright © Cassell 1995

Distributed in the United States by
Sterling Publishing Co. Inc.
387 Park Avenue South, New York, NY 10016-8810

British Library Cataloguing-in-Publication Data
A catalogue record for this book is available from the British Library.

ISBN 0 304-34810-4

All rights reserved. No part of this book may be reproduced or transmitted in any form or
by any means, electronic or mechanical, including photocopying, recording or any
information storage and retrieval system, without prior permission in writing from the
copyright holder and Publisher.

Printed and bound in Spain by Bookprint S.L.

CONTENTS

✴

INTRODUCTION

✳

*A*s designers who enjoy working with different methods and materials, we find it intriguing that the tremendous interest generated over the last few years in paint effects and stencilling in the home favours some areas and almost completely neglects others. In *Print Style* we have tried to redress the balance; we look not only at walls and furniture, but also at other elements that play an equal, if not more important, role in achieving a satisfying environment.

We have focused our attention on simple but highly versatile techniques of applying pattern to textiles and other surfaces, where applicable. We hope to dispel any misgivings that printing techniques are more difficult or expensive than painting techniques. We are all familiar with the story of how Laura Ashley began to build her empire by printing simple textiles on the kitchen table; whether true or false it is undoubtedly possible, and all the techniques we describe in this book can be printed easily in the home, for the home. We demonstrate this using a wide variety of different products and designs.

The methods that we describe in *Print Style* are practical, uncomplicated, inexpensive and versatile. For instance, everything in the picture on the front of the book, the curtain, the bedspread, the cushions and even the

A BACKDROP OF GARDEN FLOWERS
IN ONE OF OUR EARLIER GARDENS MAKES A LOVELY
SETTING FOR THESE HANDPRINTED RESIST-DYED FABRICS.

walls, has been printed using nothing more than a potato. Potato printing may be slow but it is a wonderfully cheap and versatile form of printing onto paper, cloth and walls. We have also found this method to be extremely useful for experimenting with new ideas. Silkscreen printing, on the other hand, has developed into one of the most highly sophisticated and efficient methods of printing in existence. However, the costly process involved in making it efficient for large-scale production makes it less useful for practical application in the home unless used as shown in this book, with resists or paper stencils.

As our own work develops we have found ourselves becoming more and more attracted to the 'small is beautiful' concept. We are interested in what can be achieved simply and without great expenditure. This is possibly a reaction to the fact that printed fabrics, for instance, are now easily available, but somehow many of the essential elements seem to be missing from commercially produced cloths. Often the quality and character of the cloth or the design have been diluted or dulled with super-efficient methods of production.

Printing, as opposed to drawing or painting, is really about duplicating an image, selecting a pattern, and then deciding on the printing method to be employed and the surface to be printed. It is a fascinating and rewarding craft and each method described here offers unlimited possibilities and possesses its own unique characteristics. These methods can also be combined to offer even more variations. Some of the methods are quick to execute, some are slow; some lend themselves to printing certain objects rather than others while many can be

used to print a great variety of surfaces. There is enormous scope for experimentation. *Print Style* is not intended to be a manual of everything that is possible, but an exciting introduction and a colourful insight into the methods of printing that we have found to be most relevant to simple techniques for home use.

ALTHOUGH MACHINE-PRINTED, INTERESTINGLY THE COLOUR SEPARATIONS FOR OUR TULIP RANGES OF FABRICS HAVE BEEN HAND-SPONGED AND THIS PHOTOGRAPH SHOWS THE CLOTH ON A SOFA AND PLASTICIZED AS A TABLE CLOTH WITH BUTTERCUPS.

AN EXTREMELY EARLY COLLECTION OF SPRING WILD FLOWERS ON OUR GREEN DORSET DELFT FABRIC,
DEVELOPED TO GO WITH ONE OF OUR CERAMIC RANGES.

PRINTING: THE TECHNIQUES

The printing techniques we describe in this book range from the extremely simple to the more complicated. Potato printing could hardly be more basic, yet we show how effective this technique can be. Screenprinting and resist dyeing are more demanding – even so, the materials are reasonably priced, sufficiently so for it to be worthwhile experimenting for the fun of it. We have deliberately kept the techniques to the minimum range of methods which will genuinely produce interesting and stylish results. The more you practise, the more confident you will become with the techniques and materials, and the freer you will be to create and express your own ideas.

BASICS OF DYEING AND PRINTING

At least 5000 years ago people had learned to colour fabrics using natural pigments. Most of the dyes, derived from plants, were not colour fast in water or sunlight. One exception was indigo, a plant dye that produces a permanent shade of blue, and in this book we show how to produce patterned fabrics using this ancient dyestuff.

The secret of 'fixing' dye colours in fabric was probably discovered in India about 2000BC, and by Biblical times India was famous for the variety and colour of its dyed fabrics. Patterns were originally hand painted onto fabrics: from this, the next step was to use wooden blocks to print motifs. These may have been in use in Egypt in the fourth century AD but no examples of block-printed cloth from that era survive. In twelfth-century Germany wooden blocks were used to print fabric but the stains and pigments used were not colour fast. It was not until the late seventeenth century, when the European textile industry finally learned the Indian techniques of producing colour-fast printed fabrics, that block-printed fabrics became widely available. During the Industrial Revolution the processes became ever more mechanized, and new synthetic pigments were developed which printed permanently onto fabric in an ever-widening variety of colours.

HAND PRINTING TODAY

Today synthetic dyes and specially developed pigments make it much easier for a beginner to get started. Lino blocks rather than wood blocks – which required high craft skills to

COCKEREL POTATO PRINT SHOWING
HOW THE MOTIF IS BUILT UP USING PARTS OF
POTATOES AS PRINTING BLOCKS.

offer a brief overview of the techniques covered by this book.

POTATO PRINTING

This is the simplest of all printing techniques, yet surprisingly varied in its applications. Quite simply, a pattern is cut from a potato, which is then used to print directly on to paper, fabric or a solid surface of any kind. Cheap, effective, and easy to learn, potato prints deserve to be liberated from the nursey school. For a full treatment of this technique, see the section beginning on page 44.

carve – and the invention of silkscreen printing have brought the possibility of learning how to print by hand to the hobbyist as well as the craftworker. Thus before going into detail, we

'SWANS',

AN EARLY LINO PRINT OF OURS, TOGETHER WITH THE CUT LINO BLOCKS, CUTTING TOOLS,
ROLLER AND TUBES OF INK.

LINO BLOCK PRINTING

Linoleum, or 'lino', was designed to cover floors, but also proved a boon to the hand printer. A pattern is cut into a prepared block of lino, then loaded with ink or pigment and applied direct to paper or fabric. As in the case of potato printing, the materials are cheap enough to encourage practice and experiment. This technique is covered in detail in pages 62–79.

SILK SCREEN

This printing method requires thorough preparation. The screen is a square or oblong of fine-gauge gauze stretched over a wooden frame. A stencil is mounted on the gauze and colour pigment is then forced through the mesh by a rubber spreader or squeegee, so that the stencil appears in negative on the surface beneath, usually paper of fabric. By using successive stencils, carefully matched or 'registered', it is possible to build up a complex motif in a number of colours. More detailed information can be found on pages 80–102.

ABOVE: SILK SCREEN PRINTING. HERE THE PAPER STENCILS OF THE ANTELOPE MOTIF CAN BE CLEARLY SEEN. BELOW: THE SILK-SCREEN PRINTED FABRIC SHOWING POSITIVE AND NEGATIVE ANTELOPE MOTIFS IN A RANDOM PATTERN.

RESIST DYEING

At its simplest, this technique involves applying a motif in wax or paste to the surface of a
fabric about to be dyed. (Dyeing methods are
explained in detail on pages 112–121.) After
the dyed fabric is dry, it is then washed to
remove the wax or paste (known as the resist)
to reveal the motif in negative against the new
colour. See also pages 102–111.

ABOVE: OUR RESIST INDIGO CLOTH DRYING ON A
WASHING LINE AFTER DYEING.
RIGHT: MORE RESIST-DYED FABRIC, ENHANCED
WITH OTHER HAND-PRINTING TECHNIQUES,
SHOWING THE RANGE AND VARIETY POSSIBLE WITH
HOME PRINT STYLE.

DESIGN CONSIDERATIONS

✳

Ꮍou may have a very clear idea of how you want to use prints, but you will have to consider certain factors before arriving at a satisfactory and harmonious result. These factors include the means by which you achieve the final design, the surface pattern used, and the very practical considerations of time, space, money and equipment. Good design sense is based on an appreciation of all these elements.

When deciding on an interior design, it is important to consider both the aesthetic appearance of the selected style, and its functional purpose. For example, let's examine the design considerations necessary when planning a set of curtains within a room.

The first consideration will be the use of the room and its existing decorative and functional details. You will also need to consider the general proportions and aspect of the room. The length and number of curtains will be an important factor in deciding which technique could be best used to print them. In turn, the technique selected will partly determine how you choose to repeat the pattern. The choice of fabric is also affected by the technique chosen. A very thick, coarse, or textured fabric is not suitable for resists, yet if you need a thick

FABRIC PELMETS ARE OFTEN USED TO PREVENT
FIREPLACES SMOKING. WE CHOSE SIMPLE
POTATO-PRINTED BOATS FOR THIS BEAUTIFUL
OLD BREAD OVEN.

curtain to exclude light or draughts and wax resist is your chosen method of applying the pattern, use a calico and then interline and line the curtain, thereby achieving both the function and decoration required.

You will need to consider the problem of the scale of the pattern in relation to the room. Do you want the pattern to be dramatic or unobtrusive? A bold pattern in a bright colour will give the room a focal point but a quieter effect is achieved if you paint the walls the same colour as the background of your fabric and then print a gentle pattern onto the cloth. The curtains will then enhance the room but not attract too much attention. You will need to consider what colours you should use; do you need warm or cool colours? Give all these points careful thought. As you experiment you

will find that the colour you choose affects the pattern. For example, you will notice striking differences if you print the same lino block in red and then in blue. This may seem obvious, but there are many subtleties and variations even within the tonal range of one colour; experiment until you have the result you are after.

As you design and make the curtains for the room, you are controlling the design decisions concerning function and decoration. Therefore you now have the ability to emphasize or reduce the importance of other features of the room using the same methods. You can extend the decoration to furniture, walls and even floors. The highly satisfying end result will be entirely original and tailored exactly to your requirements.

SOURCES OF INSPIRATION

In the room where we are writing this book we are surrounded by potential sources of inspiration. The room contains photographs, some taken in our local market, of geese, rabbits, poultry, flowers, ducklings poking their heads out of a basket; others are of our daughter on an old-fashioned merry-go-round, a friend's horse, ducks in the garden, traction engines, soldiers, tractors, seagulls, boats. Lining the walls, there are collections of magazines gathered over the years, rows of books, more photographs, sketch books and folders of ideas. All homes have memorabilia like this somewhere and there is no shortage of potential source material. However, what you do with it and how you use it is very rarely completely arbitrary; you will usually have reasons for choosing the various elements of your design, certain criteria which influence your choice of pattern and image.

The single most important element governing this choice is likely to be the function of the item you are decorating. Combined with this consideration will be the questions of personal taste and aesthetic balance, as well as the choice of technique. Each technique has its part to play as a potential source for inspiration. Ironically, this is as much to do with the limitations of each technique as much as its possibilities.

There are many ways of approaching the design considerations of matching patterns to your rooms and lifestyle. You may, for example, be inspired by a bowl of cherries and wish to create a pattern for printing onto fabric from it. After some hard work and a great deal of

OPPOSITE AND ABOVE:
IT IS EASY TO DEVELOP DECORATIVE IDEAS FROM
VERY ORDINARY DOMESTIC SURROUNDINGS.

fun you will have a length of cloth. Now, what do you do with it? We would suggest you take it from room to room, drape it over chairs, up at windows, fold it over books, in fact anything you can think of. Very quickly, you will see what arrangement your particular design lends itself to. Alternatively, to avoid the expense of printing cloth, in the first instance you could print a sheet of paper or even, as we have with our boat print on page 74, create a lino-cut picture to experiment with the image.

THE FLOWERS ON THE OPPOSITE PAGE WERE VERY QUICKLY PHOTOGRAPHED IN OUR GARDEN
AND POTATOES WERE USED TO MAKE THE PATTERNS. THIS PARTICULAR EXERCISE TOOK NO LONGER THAN
A MORNING, AND WE COULD CERTAINLY HAVE DONE FURTHER WORK ON THE THEMES.
THE WHOLE POINT OF THE EXERCISE WAS TO SHOW HOW EASY IT IS TO GET STARTED WITH THE SIMPLEST
OF DECORATIVE TECHNIQUES.

Matching patterns to the home environment is so much a matter of personal taste that you can take your inspiration from the objects around you or alternatively you can scour magazines and old books until you find a style that you find pleasing. If you are working from an idea in a magazine, try not to copy the look exactly. Analyse what it is about the image that you like. For instance, a piece of lovely Italian china was the starting point for a recent design commission where the beautiful oranges and greens used in the china inspired us to use colours that were different from our usual favourite blues and wilder reds.

There is a school of thought that rightly or wrongly advocates that the gap between conceiving an idea in your head and being able to execute it should be as short and trouble-free as possible and that the creative process should not be inhibited by lack of equipment and facilities. The problem is that there is a very delicate balance and it is important to learn and understand a technique before you can use it constructively, exploiting all its possibilities. This is not achieved by presenting it in its most sophisticated and efficient form. For example, we do not learn to weave on a Jacquard loom in preference to a two-shaft table loom or learn to knit on a computer-aided Jacquard circular jersey knitting machine before acquiring some hand knitting skills.

It is a fact that thousands of beautiful and innovative artefacts have been made in the past and are still being produced all over the world in conditions and with equipment that we would probably consider far from ideal. The problem is, perhaps, that in the western world we have become so used to everything being easily available that we prefer to buy something rather than to make it for ourselves. The tide is undoubtedly turning, however; there is renewed interest in crafts skills and we are happy to try our hand at producing items at home, rather than buying them in a shop at great expense.

We offer some practical and enjoyable techniques, yet perhaps the most difficult part is getting started. However, once you have defined your objective, the imagery and colours will invariably follow. So start with a simple technique: cut a potato in half, cut a pattern and start printing.

PATTERN AND REPEAT

In order to execute your ideas as patterns you must first consider the repeat. The basis of all

pattern is repetition and almost any motif repeated in an organized way will produce a pattern. Although we are extremely fond of random designs, like our zoo animal prints where the animals are repeatedly moved around on the cloth simply by placing them where they look best (see page 127), there are more formal methods which are not quite as arbitrary. Once you have understood the general principles, constructing patterns and making them work on the printing medium will be extremely satisfying and enjoyable. In this book an understanding of how to put pattern into repeat is particularly important because we describe simple methods of applying pattern to surfaces which are pre-dominantly fabrics. All the methods we describe involve applying the pattern within a relatively small printing unit compared to the size of the area to be covered. Therefore your motifs should be organized within that area to achieve the most suitable and harmonious arrangement on the cloth. For this reason, the shape and size of the motif are of great importance.

ABOVE RIGHT:
CAN YOU IDENTIFY THE REPEATED BLOCK PATTERN HERE? FOR A CLUE, LOOK AT THE PHOTOGRAPH ON PAGE 62–3. A SIMPLE GEOMETRIC DIVISION OF THE AREA TO BE PRINTED IS ESSENTIAL IF ACCURATE REGISTRATION AND PRINTING IS TO BE ACHIEVED.

RIGHT AND FAR RIGHT: SIMPLE DIVISIONS OF A SURFACE INTO SQUARES OR DIAMONDS FORM A BASIS FOR PATTERNS. THE DIVISION INTO SQUARES ALLOWS FOR A LARGER MOTIF. THE DIVISION INTO DIAMONDS REQUIRES A SMALLER MOTIF.

Geometric division

The shape is usually constructed on a geometrical basis because it is a relatively simple matter to divide the material into equal parts by lines intersecting either horizontally and vertically or diagonally, the resulting units being either squares, rectangles or diamonds. The size of the motif is determined by the width of the material that you are printing. This means that for a fabric that is 90 cm (36 in) wide the unit size could be of any measurement that fits equally into the total width. Each method of printing that we describe in *Print Style* has a size limitation, and this is particularly applicable in the case of a lino block, where there is an optimum size that you can hold comfortably when printing.

Selecting the image

Next, you should establish whether the motif or pattern repeats successfully. The square or rectangular unit is probably the most commonly used shape. A successful repeated design achieves a satisfactory union between each successive printing of the unit. In order to do this the pattern within the unit should join not only on each side but also at the top and bottom when it is printed. Without these considerations the division between each printing of the unit would be seen clearly as vertical and horizontal lines. At this stage we strongly advise you to experiment, a process which can be enjoyable as well as useful. Start by putting

THESE FLOWERS, STRIPES AND CHECKS WERE ALL PRODUCED WITH POTATO PRINTS. WE'VE HAD TO SHOW THEM RATHER LESS THAN LIFE SIZE, BUT YOU CAN EASILY ENLARGE THEM WITH A XEROX MACHINE. THE SIZE OF EACH MOTIF IS LIMITED ONLY BY THE SIZE OF THE POTATO!

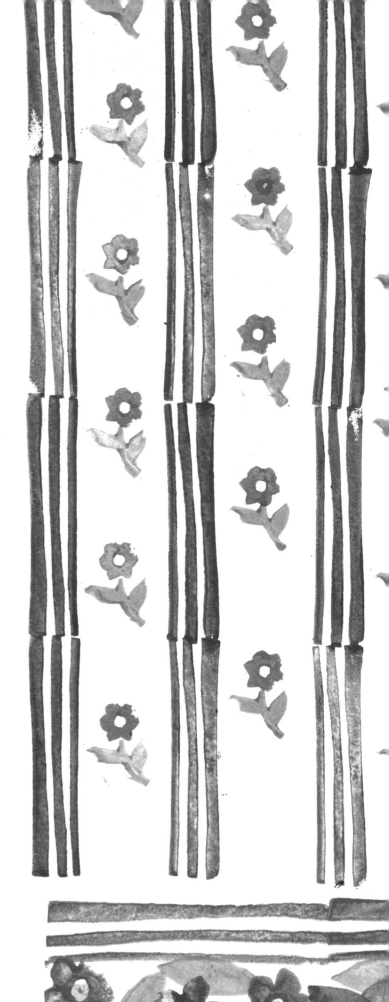

a potato print into repeat. Cut the potatoes into squares and simple patterns. In the first instance do not worry whether or not the motif repeats, just observe the results and see what happens as the shapes progress across the paper, how they leave blank areas or come too close to one another.

Creating the pattern

Now you can start to be specific; take an idea,

motif or sketch that interests you and decide on the size that you would like to print it. Divide a large sheet of paper into the shape of printing unit you prefer and gradually work up your pattern within the squares, rectangles or diamonds. The key to success is to work out how the motif can be best placed within this grid to disguise the boundary lines of the unit, thus creating a pattern. Tracing paper is invaluable for this exercise because you are able to see by moving parts of the unit into another whether it will repeat and also what adjustments you will need to make to achieve a repeating pattern. If you have access to a photocopier you will find it very useful at this stage.

Another method which will show you if your pattern will repeat and help you make any necessary adjustments is as follows, as shown here: Cut a tracing of your pattern unit into four squares by cutting down the centre and across the centre. Now change the position of the four squares. Put the bottom squares onto the top and change over the sides as in the diagram. This new arrangement of the squares will give you the information you need. If you take a tracing of it, you can

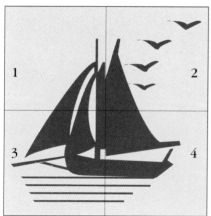
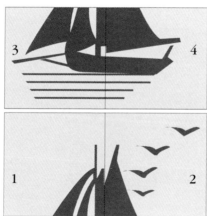
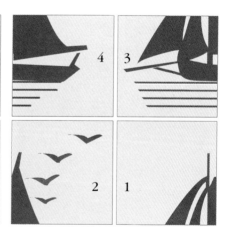

make sure that the lines match up, concealing the mechanical edge of the pattern and allowing it to flow smoothly. The boat lino cut on page 23 is an example of this.

As you become familiar with the process of repeat it becomes apparent that the geometrical division of the cloth necessary to define the unit can also be utilized as a feature in the pattern. This can take two forms. The first is where the pattern is directly evolved from a

geometric shape, for example, a square, diamond or circle; the second is the number of different ways in which the unit can be placed within the geometrical division of the cloth.

Alternatively, you may have designed a motif but do not want to repeat it formally yet you do want to organize its position on the cloth. In this case you may want to use one of the traditional methods of organizing repeats which include:

PRINCIPLES OF PATTERN: THE HALF-DROP REPEAT. IT'S EASY TO SEE THAT THE TWO COCKERELS IN THE MIDDLE COULD BE MOVED UP TO ALIGN WITH THE OTHERS. THIS WOULD BE CALLED THE 'FULL-DROP REPEAT' OR 'DIAPER'.

The border
The random repeat
*The half-drop repeat (in which the print unit is
dropped by one half of a unit)*
*The full-drop repeat, sometimes referred to as
a diaper*

When you come to printing your cloth in
repeats it is very useful to have some indication on the cloth as to where you should place
your screen or block. We recommend marking
out a grid with tailor's chalk, or by stretching a
black cotton thread (if the fabric is pale) as
tightly as possible and securing it with pins at
the end of the fabric.

HERE THE FULL-DROP PATTERN HAS BEEN ADAPTED
TO MAKE A BORDER.

THESE PAGES SHOW A NUMBER OF DECORATIVE MOTIFS ARRANGED IN DIFFERENT KINDS OF PATTERNS.
USE A PHOTOCOPIER TO MULTIPLY THE ELEMENTS, THEN CUT THEM UP AND EXPERIMENT WITH DIFFERENT
TYPES OF ARRANGEMENT.

EQUIPMENT

✳

$\mathcal{T}$he equipment needed for carrying out the techniques in this book is relatively basic and inexpensive. Second-hand shops can be a good source for some of the domestic utensils. Some methods require more specialist items so we recommend that you start with an extremely simple technique such as potato printing and gradually work through the others. If you do this you can buy, make or find the right tool for the job over a longer period of time. We have provided here a list of what we consider to be essential equipment.

The printing board

The most important item is a suitable surface on which to print the cloth, and you will need to prepare a padded board specifically for this purpose. The board needs to be soft and waterproof. You can make a portable print board, which can be used when and where you wish, from a piece of blockboard approximately 60 x 150 cm (24 x 60 in), large enough for printing a width of furnishing fabric. Stretch two or even three layers of thick woollen blanket over the board and attach them to the edge of the board using short, large-headed nails. Stretch PVC-covered cloth over the blankets and nail down. The board is now ready for use. If possible choose a plain, unpatterned

A REPRESENTATIVE SELECTION OF THE EQUIPMENT YOU WILL NEED TO CARRY OUT THE TECHNIQUES DESCRIBED IN THIS BOOK. QUITE A LOT IS LIKELY TO BE FOUND AROUND THE HOME, BUT SOME — SUCH AS THE SCALPELS, STAPLE GUN, SETSQUARE AND SO ON — WILL HAVE TO BE SPECIALLY BOUGHT FROM YOUR LOCAL ART SUPPLIES SHOP.

YOU WILL NEED TO MAKE A PRINTING BOARD TO SUPPORT THE FABRIC DURING PRINTING. THIS IS EASILY MADE FROM A WOODEN BASE ON WHICH IS TACKED TWO LAYERS OF THICK WOOLLEN BLANKET AND A TOP LAYER OF WATERPROOF MACINTOSH CLOTH.

cloth for your waterproof surface. This method of making a printing board provides a firm but soft washable surface onto which the fabric can be secured using masking tape.

Printing pads

These are used in lino block fabric printing to hold the pigment dyestuff. They can be regarded as smaller versions of the printing board and are made in the same way. For details see page 68.

Blocks of lino

See pages 65–66 for advice on preparing lino blocks.

Containers

These should be airtight and can be glass jars or plastic containers. These are needed to store dye and paints. Do remember to label them.

Plastic bowls and buckets

A selection of different sizes for mixing and washing up.

Plastic dustbins for cold water dyeing

Galvanized or stainless steel bucket

For hot water dyeing and wax removal dairy buckets are available from farm suppliers.

Iron, preferably cordless

A chopping board

Fine craft or art knives
Used for cutting stencils.

Set of gouges for lino cutting

Carbon paper
Useful for transferring designs to lino.

Useful extras
Brown tape, masking tape, pins, glue, gums, short nails with large heads. Staple, gum, hammer, saw and set square.

Tongs

Apron and rubber gloves
Although we would not describe any of the chemicals and dyestuffs used in the book as dangerous, all chemicals and dyes should be treated carefully and with caution. They should be stored away from food, medicines and other household chemicals, preferably in a locked cupboard. Even when we recommend using very ordinary domestic or household items they should be used exclusively for printing or dyeing to avoid any mistakes being made. Flour, salt, wax, whatever – keep it separate. Be very strict about this as it is possible for all manner of potentially dangerous substances to become confused with other household items. This can be hazardous, especially if there are children about. Be sure to label everything. Use separate measuring and weighing tools, as many of the items used for textile printing are the same as those required for cooking – do please keep them separate.

Wax
An electric heating pan with built in thermometer for wax resist.

Rulers and tape measures

Thermometer

Glass or plastic measuring jug

Old spoons for mixing
Stainless steel spoons are best, but plastic will do.

Paper kitchen towels
Useful for every occasion.

A good strong kitchen knife
For cutting the potatoes in half.

PAPERS AND FABRIC

✳

PAPERS

There is a wide range of papers suitable for
printing and the simplest print will look all the
better for appearing on the right paper —
which need not at all be the most expensive.
In fact, painters have always experimented
with different papers — Turner, for example,
used wrapping and writing papers for his
watercolours, while David Hockney used hand-
made paper for a recent series of swimming-
pool prints.

Machine-made cartridge papers make up the
standard art-shop range, but are considered by
some to be very dull. At the other end, the
most heavily textured (and expensive) hand-
made papers are virtually useless for our printing techniques as the colour goes patchy.
Between the two extremes, however, are many
different types, textures and colours which you
should experiment with to see which suits your
purposes best. Even choosing from a selection
of white papers you will be surprised at how
many whites there are, along with as many
variations in weight and surface: smooth white
card, for instance, can give especially clear and
luminous results with lino-block prints.

The best quality papers have always been

YOU WILL NEED TO TAKE EXPERT ADVICE FROM
YOUR ART SUPPLIER AS TO WHICH PAPERS ARE MOST
SUITABLE FOR TAKING PRINTS. EVEN SO, YOU WILL
BE SURPRISED AT THE RANGE OF TEXTURES AND
COLOURS AVAILABLE, AND HOW EFFECTIVE THEY ARE
COMBINED WITH SIMPLE PRINTS TO MAKE CARDS AND
STATIONERY FOR ALL OCCASIONS.

WE WERE LUCKY ENOUGH TO DISCOVER A RANGE OF FRENCH HAND-MADE PAPERS TO TAKE OUR SELECTION
OF LINO-BLOCK PRINTED ZOO ANIMALS.

A RATHER CAREFULLY CUT POTATO WAS USED TO PRINT THESE WRAPPING PAPERS
AS A CHEAP AND QUICK ALTERNATIVE TO SEARCHING THE STORES FOR SOMETHING
OUT OF THE ORDINARY.

manufactured from cotton fibre. The percentage of rag is the term used to define the cotton content. These papers are acid free and will therefore be particularly durable. Many mould-made, or 'laid', papers are available in rolls, useful if you are considering printing your own wallpaper or wallpaper frieze. Modern tinted papers are light-fast and hot-pressed papers have a good resistance to pressure and so are particularly suitable for lino block printing. Papers are changing all the time and bear in mind that one named batch does not always exactly resemble another. All these are good reasons to keep experimenting and do not begrudge the time you spend doing so.

A resist for paper can be made out of gelatine size or of gum arabic in its liquid form. These resists can be very useful if you use a beautiful, coloured paper and then flood it with watercolour to emulate a dyebath.

ABOVE AND LEFT:
WHEN OUR NEIGHBOUR IN NORMANDY, A LOCAL
FARMER, GAVE US A DOZEN OR TWO BOTTLES OF HIS
HOME-MADE CIDER, WE DECIDED TO CREATE THIS
HOME-MADE POTATO PRINT LABEL.

OPPOSITE:
GREETINGS CARDS AND A FRIEZE IN THE PROCESS OF
BEING POTATO PRINTED.

FABRICS

Natural fabrics are the most useful for the printing methods described in this book. For routine experimenting we use a lightweight calico but as this cloth is very high quality and a pretty colour in its natural state, we often use it for projects as well, for printing curtains, for instance. Other natural-fibre fabrics such as cottons, silks and fine wool are also suitable. Specialist fabric suppliers carry large ranges of cottons and silks in many different weights. The dress and furnishing fabric departments of stores often have suitable cottons and it is also well worth keeping an eye on the market stalls. Another source of supply are secondhand shops where you can occasionally find bundles of old linen or sheeting of excellent quality, often in very beautiful natural colours. Take care, however, if buying old cottons and linens as these fibres can rot with time and from use. Do not waste your time and effort by printing onto worn cloth and examine old linens very carefully before buying, as these wear particularly easily.

We do not recommend the use of synthetic fibres for printing with the dyes used in this book. Special dyes are available for this purpose and you should refer to a specialist book on the subject. Having said this, however, we have a 50 per cent polyester quilt cover that we resist-printed years ago and then dyed in indigo. Although paler than its cotton counterparts it is very pretty. If you really prefer a cotton/polyester mix for bedding, for example, do experiment first as the results will vary from those you would achieve on a natural fabric. Experiment not only with the printing or dyeing but also with washing and finishing to test for colour durability.

A SELECTION OF BLEACHED AND UNBLEACHED NATURAL FABRICS. CALICO, COTTON, SILK AND FINE WOOL ARE ALL SUITABLE FOR PRINTING.

Preparing fabric for printing

Whatever cloth you select, it is essential that you prepare it for printing. New cloth has its own finishing substances in it, the products

soon as we buy them so that they are ready for use.

To remove the finishing products simply put the cottons or linens in the washing machine with a small amount of non-biological washing powder or liquid and wash at 60°C (140°F). If the water in your area is very hard add a water-softening agent. Silk and wool do not take kindly to high temperatures and wool must not be agitated, or it will become felted. Hand wash silk and wool gently in a product formulated for washing wool and rinse very thoroughly. Keep the temperature hand-hot throughout the process – approximately 30°C (70°F). In the case of wool never let the water from the taps flow directly onto the cloth and do not soak. Silk tends to lose its lustre if washed in high temperatures.

Let the cloths dry naturally, on a line if possible; do not use a tumble dryer for silk or wool. A spin dryer, however, is very useful for wool as it removes the water very quickly. Once dried and ironed the cloths are ready for printing.

Fixing the design

After printing you must iron the cloth really well to fix the dye. We recommend that you keep an iron to hand at all times while printing to iron out creases and fix the dye after printing is finished. To fix the design, press with a hot iron, keeping the iron on the printed areas as long as possible without running the risk of scorching. Do not use steam. Give the finished piece another good press later on before use. We have found an ironing press to be very useful; it is not an essential piece of equipment but it does speed things up. When the dye is fixed your printed fabric is ready to made up.

used to help in the weaving and to bulk the cloth prior to sale, and it is essential to wash these out before printing or dyeing. Fabrics prepared for printing are available from fabric and dye suppliers, and these are useful if for any reason you wish to get off to a quick start. However, to make absolutely sure, we wash all fabrics that we intend to use for printing as

PIGMENTS
FOR PRINTING

✳

For printing fabric we specify pigment dyestuffs: our preferred brand is called 'Polyprint', a two-part system consisting of a highly concentrated pigment colour, and a binder, to which the colour is added.

Polyprint produce packs of pigment in different sizes. The small pack – six 60 ml (2 fl oz) jars of colour and one barrel of 2.3 litres (½ gallon) of binder – is sufficient to produce the projects described in this book.

Prepare a paste by mixing the pigment with the binder in the following proportions:

Deep shade: 10 parts pigment 90 parts binder
Medium shade: 4 parts pigment 96 parts binder
Pale shade: 1 part pigment   99 parts binder

If you are tackling a large item such as curtains record the proportions used and mix to the same proportions when you run out, rather than mixing a huge amount at once. Pigment when mixed with binder does last well if covered but we prefer to mix in small quantities, recording the formula. Remember that silkscreen printing uses far more binder than other methods, so you may need to order extra binder.

Fix using a hot iron, following the manufacturer's instructions. Use the hottest iron setting for the particular fabric and iron several times until the pigment is thoroughly fixed.

A SELECTION OF PIGMENT DYESTUFFS USED FOR PRINTING ON FABRICS.

POTATO PRINTING

✳

*I*t is understandable that there is no wealth of background history associated with potato printing other than it being one of the activities we might have practised at primary school during art lessons; even then it was often considered too messy or too elementary an exercise. Yet there are few techniques for applying patterns that are as cheap and efficient and which offer so much scope for imaginative use.

The general principle of potato printing is extremely simple: a potato is cut in half and a pattern is gouged out of or cut into the soft surface, colour (usually as water based inks or dyes) is applied with an ordinary brush and the potato pattern printed onto the material to be decorated. Whatever misgivings you may have about your ability to cut a block of lino or to make a successful screen, the same doubts should not be applied to printing with potatoes. Potato printing is the ideal technique for a beginner to use to experiment with pattern and image. We have been amazed when producing the work for this book at how much has been possible and the wide range of surfaces that can be printed with so little fuss. The more potato printing you do the more you become involved. It also has the advantage that it can become a group activity: the whole family can join in.

THIS SPARKLING COLLECTION OF CARDS, FRIEZES
AND FABRICS SHOWS THE WIDELY VARYING
POSSIBILITIES OF THE HUMBLE POTATO PRINT!

POTATO-PRINTED TIE-ON COVERS FOR HOME-MADE PRESERVES ADD EXTRA CHARM TO A COUNTRY KITCHEN.
PAGES 50–51 SHOW HOW TO MAKE THE STRAWBERRY MOTIF IN STEP-BY-STEP DETAIL.
USE THE METHOD TO CREATE THE APPROPRIATE TIE-ON FOR EACH PRESERVE – MOST GARDEN FRUITS
HAVE STRONG, SIMPLE SHAPES THAT ARE EASY TO EXPERIMENT WITH.

Greetings cards are a good example of effective potato printing. It really makes a difference if you are sent a hand-made card. Why not, for instance, have a family potato printing session at Christmas to make the cards and wrapping papers much as you might have a cooking session for Christmas puddings and mince pies?

Pretty covers for bottled fruit and preserves are great fun to design and make, and are lovely to look at. The confidence and the enjoyment that you will gain from making these projects can only encourage you to go on to print cushions and even curtains.

While we are fond of using potatoes there are many other natural and manufactured materials that can also be used for successful printing. We have developed a range of resist fabrics that are printed in Malaysia. These fabrics are printed from copper strips soldered onto an iron base. In parts of Pakistan small terracotta stamps are used, in Africa the famous adinka cloths of the Ashanti are printed using patterned stamps made from pieces of old calabash, the gourd-like shell of the fruit of the calabash tree (also known as the bottle gourd). Be prepared to experiment and improvise – the unexpected may provide an excellent printing block.

Among the objects from which you can select printing blocks are cut and uncut natural and synthetic sponges. Plaster of Paris, clay, corrugated cardboard, polystyrene, cotton reels, cork, even wire netting and leaves can be inked up and printed. Although many of these will be quickly dismissed as impractical, the knowledge and experience gained from trying them out is invaluable in formulating your ideas and designs.

SELECTING THE POTATO

It would be ridiculous to make too much fuss about the selection of the most suitable potato for printing but there are, nevertheless, some practical considerations. Generally, large potatoes are more useful than small ones. A small potato restricts the size of the pattern and is also extremely difficult to hold.

Potatoes are not difficult to obtain at any time of the year but the main growing and harvesting season runs from mid-summer through to late winter. Do spend some time selecting the right shape potato for printing your design; this is particularly important if the design is long and large. When, for example, we select a natural sponge from the chemist's shop, the assistants are amazed as we ponder over each one examining its characteristics. We use a great many sponges in our ceramic work and each one imparts its own particular character. Now the market stallholders are astonished as we ponder over the potatoes, selecting each

one individually and then buying in great quantities. Fortunately we live in a vegetable-producing area and have a good choice. Once you have amassed a suitable selection of potatoes we recommend three ways of printing them.

PRINTING

Method 1

Cut the potato in half, regardless of its shape and size. Cut your designs into each half and then, if printing on fabric brush dyestuff onto the potato and press down firmly onto the cloth; if printing on paper, use gouache or water paint. We have found that water-based inks and dyes are most suitable. Very simple patterns, such as lines or curves that do not repeat, are most suitable and produce charming, traditional patterns. The results are often reminiscent of old book papers of the 1930s.

Method 2

This method is a more organized and formal method of printing. In this instance larger potatoes are useful. Cut the potato in half, then cut the half into a square, rectangle or diamond. In this method designs can be worked out and cut that will definitely repeat as the block is printed. The design need not be complicated.

Method 3

Many of our potato prints are produced using this method and it will help you to understand the process if you study the pictures of the birds in the potato print illustrations on page 58. To produce these, on paper we drew a very simple formalized bird on a twig, separating out the main elements – body, tail, head, twig and leaf. We then coloured the areas of the design using crayons. Each component part was then treated as a separate element in the design. The body or tail, for example, could be as large or as long as the potato from which you intend to print. When all these parts were put together the completed image was far larger than would have been possible if printed with a single potato. If you are lucky enough to find some extremely large potatoes the design can be very large indeed.

TRANSFERRING THE DESIGN TO THE POTATOES

To transfer the elements of the design onto the potatoes you will need some thin paper, such as layout paper. Trace over the original design and, using a fine craft knife, cut out each part. When you have done this mark each part with a pencil to show which is the right way up. Cut the potato in half and lay the shapes on the cut surface using the craft knife. The paper shape acts as a template to guide you when you cut the design. Cut as deeply as possible because you will need to be able to hold the potato easily when printing.

BASIC EQUIPMENT FOR POTATO PRINTING.

The paper templates can be used again but it is a good idea to also cut the component parts of your design out of stencil paper which will last longer. The cut potato will only really last a day or so in constant use. The pressure, although light, required to print each part, together with the repeated application of pigment or paint, will slowly contribute to the deterioration of the images, so you will need to use the paper templates to cut more potatoes.

PRINTING WITH THE POTATOES

The process of printing with potatoes is straightforward and the same whether you are using paint or dye. Having removed your paper template (if you have used one) apply the pigment or paint to the printing surface of the potato with a soft, flat brush. Place the potato in position and gently press onto the cloth or paper. Brush more colour onto the surface of the potato between printings and repeat until your project is completed. We prefer to print each component separately, by this we mean that we will, for example, print all the bodies of the birds first and then move on to the tail, and then the other parts, only printing one item at a time. This way the different colours are not being used at the same time and the chance of making a mistake is minimized.

We find it useful, if printing a design such as the strawberry print (see pages 50–51), to use coloured paper templates to assist in the composition. Here the overall design is constructed from small potato blocks as it is difficult to compose the pattern as you print. This is particularly important in the strawberry pattern as the leaves must be spaced far enough apart to leave sufficient gaps between them in which to print the

FABRIC POTATO PRINTED WITH THE STRAWBERRY-AND-LEAF MOTIF USING METHOD 3 (SEE OVERLEAF). CAREFUL ATTENTION TO PATTERN BUILDING CAN CREATE A WONDERFULLY LIVELY EFFECT FROM BASIC ELEMENTS.

strawberry. To do this we cut out approximate shapes of the completed leaves in green paper and the strawberry in pink paper. We then laid the templates on the cloth to compose the overall design, moving the templates as we progressed.

Keep your printing area well-organized and clean. This is very important and applies to all the techniques described in the book, but particularly to potato printing where your fingers will quickly become covered with the printing medium and fingerprints and small spots of colour will begin to appear very quickly. We recommend keeping a bowl or bucket of warm soapy water and rag or kitchen roll always to hand.

1 Start by working out your chosen design in pencil. When you are happy with this, use a craft knife to cut around the individual elements which will make up the design. Always make sure that the blade you use is very sharp to avoid snagging the paper.

2 Cut your selected potato in half using a sharp knife and with some thin paper, such as layout paper, trace over the original design and lay these on to the surface of the potato.

3 With the craft knife cut around the shapes, cutting as deeply as possible which will enable you to hold the potato easily when printing.

4 Remove your paper stencil and apply the pigment or paint to the printing surface of the potato with a soft, flat brush.

5 Using a lino cutting tool work out where the veins of the leaf will fall and then gently 'gouge' them out. When using any sharp implements always remember to cut away from your body, not towards it.

6 Now you are ready to start printing. Place the potato in position and gently press it down on to the cloth. Repeat this as many times as you wish, brushing more colour on to the surface between printing.

7 Switching to the stem of the leaf, repeat the previous process.

8 The next element of the design is the strawberry. Once again carefully cut out the holes which will give the impression of the textured surface of the strawberry, then apply the colour and print as before.

9 The final part of the design is the strawberry's husk. This is again printed in the same way. To avoid any smudges from appearing on the cloth make sure that you keep a bowl of soapy water and a rag close to hand.

A POTATO-PRINTED BLUE CHECK TABLECLOTH WILL TAKE A WHILE TO PRINT,
BUT IS THE ESSENCE OF COUNTRY STYLE.

We are fond of printed checks, even though woven checks are considered superior, perhaps as a throwback to the supremacy of weaving over the years. The blue-and-white check tablecloth, simply printed with a potato, is one of our favourites. It reminds us of an old black and white photograph taken years ago, which depicts a bowl of eggs on a checked cloth. We decided to print a tablecloth and napkins using this image for inspiration.

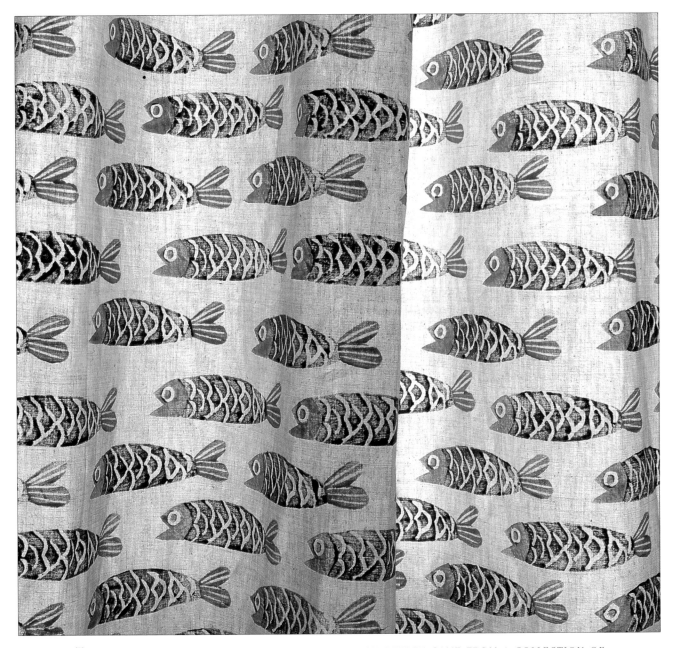

THE INSPIRATION FOR THIS EXTREMELY SIMPLE FISH DESIGN CAME FROM A COLLECTION OF
NEPALESE HAND-PRINTED PAPERS. ALTHOUGH NOTHING LIKE THE ORIGINAL, OUR POTATO-PRINTED MOTIF
PRESERVES THE SIMPLE, NAÏVE STYLE WE WISHED TO EMULATE.

We first saw our Nepalese fish on some eastern block-printed papers. We converted the motif to a potato print in three sections – head, body and tail – and used it in our aquamarine hall, which we use for dining. The many doors and corridors off the hall needed draught-excluding curtains, and we thought that the style suited the rattan chairs placed near the wood-burning stove.

LEFT AND ABOVE:
WE PRINTED OUR FISH ON OLD COTTON SHEET MATERIAL, WHICH IS HEAVY ENOUGH TO MAKE A
DRAUGHT-EXCLUDING CURTAIN (ABOVE) FOR OUR DINING-ROOM/HALL. THE RATTAN CHAIR BY THE
WOOD-BURNING STOVE SEEMED TO MATCH THE ORIENTAL FEEL OF OUR FISH.

BIRD BEDROOM

✶

Child's Coverlet

The room shown on the front of the book is used by visiting children, some of them past the baby nursery stage. The bed in the room needed a coverlet for which we designed a bird pattern, pretty but not too babyish. The imagery and quality we were obtaining in our experiments with potatoes seemed perfectly suited to this project, particularly when printed on our much-loved calico. When we had completed the coverlet we decided to extend the design to the curtains and walls, producing a joyful pattern of brightly coloured birds which stand out like jewels.

You will need a piece of calico, and the same amount of flame-retardant polyester wadding. After the design is complete and the patchwork made up, sandwich the wadding between the design and the backing fabric before finishing off the coverlet.

1 As potato printing is on a relatively small scale, cut the fabric into squares for printing and then reassemble them later as a patchwork.

2 Choose your design and cut it into the potato halves. Experiment by printing on squares of paper and then move on to printing on spare squares of calico. Keep the discarded fabric squares: these can be made into patchwork cushions later or kept in your sample folder. When you are happy with the design and the repeat, print onto the squares that will form the coverlet.

3 Leave the squares to dry, then fix according to the manufacturer's instructions for the dyestuff medium. Join the squares together. Measure a piece of fabric for the border and fold it and print the border design along the folded edge.

Bird curtains

This room has shutters at the window so curtains are not essential, but they would enhance the effect of the design, particularly as the room is used by children and so needs to look light and welcoming. We decided on a long curtain as there is an awkward shelf below the window, positioned there to stop the rain driven against the window by southerly winds from falling on the floor when the windows are open.

The thought of potato-printing a large area of fabric to produce the curtains was rather daunting; the project would have been ideal for silkscreening or dyeing but the effect would have been different. Before starting we made sure that we had enough potatoes of the correct size to print the whole area, as the duration of the printing would last longer than a single potato.

WE DECIDED TO DECORATE THIS GUEST BEDROOM ENTIRELY WITH POTATO PRINTS. EVEN SO, WE WERE PLEASANTLY SURPRISED AT THE RANGE OF EFFECTS WE FOUND IT POSSIBLE TO ACHIEVE.

When tackling an area of this size, you need to find a way of keeping the cloth clean and off the floor as you work. The solution we recommend is to roll the cloth onto a large cardboard roll (ideally an old fabric roll). Keep the rolled fabric near you as you work, and, starting from the top, roll out a piece ready to print. If necessary, secure the fabric to the printing board using masking tape. As you complete each section, allow it to dry and push the fabric away from you before unrolling the next portion. If you are in a hurry or the prints are taking a while to dry, you can speed up the drying process by using a hair dryer. If you need the printing space for other activities, you can store the fabric rolled up like this in between sessions (having made sure it is dry first, of course).

ABOVE AND ABOVE RIGHT: THE BASIC MOTIF OF THE BEDROOM IS THIS CHEERFUL SONGBIRD PERCHED ON A TWIG. ON THE LEFT YOU CAN SEE THE POTATO PIECES FOR EACH OF THE ELEMENTS, THE HEAD AND BODY, THE TAIL, THE TWIG AND THE LEAF. THE LEGS WERE PAINTED IN WITH A FINE BRUSH.

WE DID QUITE A BIT OF DESIGN WORK ON THE FLOWER MOTIFS FOR THE WALLS BEFORE SETTLING ON THE SIMPLIFIED DAISY PATTERN ON THE RIGHT, WITH JUST THE TWO ELEMENTS, THE PETAL AND CIRCULAR 'EYE' OF THE FLOWER.

1 Measure the window where you wish to hang the curtains, and calculate enough fabric to include gathers and hems. Thick, coarse cotton sheeting is a good choice here. Lay the fabric flat on the floor and place different size plates on it until you are happy with the distribution of the images. We used plates that were 25 cm (10 in) in circumference for our design, and decided to add more foliage in the background to alter the emphasis of the pattern. Once you have decided on the positioning of the images, space the plates evenly and draw round them in soft pencil.

2 The birds are printed using Method 3 (see page 48), so cut paper templates for each portion of the design and follow the technique for this method. Apply each colour separately and allow it to dry before adding the next part of the design. When the design is complete, fix the dyestuff according to the manufacturer's instructions.

The walls

Under the window shelf is an area of rough plaster. We painted this with two coats of emulsion paint, and then potato-printed on the flowers using gouache. When the design was dry, we added a coat of acrylic varnish. If you want to decorate a wall in this way, and you find that you do not like the design, the images can be washed off before varnish is applied. Alternatively, you can paint different designs onto paper first and then, when you are happy with the effect, print them directly onto the wall using emulsion paints, following the paper pattern as a guide.

Do remember that potatoes should be printed with water-based paints so bear this in mind when selecting paint for printing. We used gouache for the walls, which were already emulsioned white. Once we had decided how to position the birds and how far apart they should be, we cut a triangular template, the sides of which were the distance between the birds. We marked the walls where they were to be placed using chalk. We proceeded according to Method 3 (see pages 49–52) as when printing the curtains, printing the bodies first and the other details separately.

(see pages 49–52)

BELOW AND RIGHT:
ONE SPIN-OFF FROM OUR INITIAL DESIGN WORK
FOR THE BEDROOM WAS THIS COUNTRY-STYLE
FLOWER-AND-VASE DESIGN.
THIS COULD WORK WELL AS A SINGLE MOTIF
ON A PAINTED WOODEN BEDHEAD OR CUPBOARD,
BUT ALSO TRANSLATED EFFECTIVELY ONTO
UNBLEACHED CALICO.

THE CURTAIN FROM THE BEDROOM, SHOWING HOW THE PATTERN WORKS.

BLOCK
PRINTING

✳

*B*lock printing was the first mechanical method of applying pattern to a textile surface. The general principle is straightforward, and consists of drawing or transferring a design onto the surface of a block of wood and then cutting away all those parts of the surface which are not to be printed, leaving the design standing out in relief. Ink or dyestuff is then applied to this surface and the block pressed onto the material to be printed. There are two methods of producing the image: either the design is cut away and the background is left in relief, or the background is cut away leaving the design in relief. A separate block is required for each colour used in the design. Printing blocks in Europe were traditionally made from fairly hard and close-grained woods such as holly, box, lime, pear, plane and sycamore.

There are certain factors to consider when block-printing using wooden designs. It is very difficult to cut fine, delicate patterns onto a hard wood block without causing the wood grain to split; also, a delicate pattern would not withstand the wear and tear of repeated printing. For this reason, block-printed designs, which undoubtedly have an unsurpassed beauty, are usually relatively bold and simple.

LINO BLOCKS CAN BE USED TO PRINT PAPER OR FABRIC. HERE IS A SELECTION OF THE BLOCKS WE USE TO PRINT OUR MOTIFS, ALONG WITH THE INK PAD (BOTTOM LEFT) AND LINO-CUTTING GOUGES.

COURTESY WILLIAM MORRIS MUSEUM, LONDON

HAND-BLOCKED WALLPAPER BY WILLIAM MORRIS, DESIGNED IN 1883. THIS BEAUTIFUL PATTERN, CALLED 'STRAWBERRY THIEF', SHOWS WOOD-BLOCK PRINTING AT ITS MOST SKILFUL.

The design and the size of the block must be chosen in relation to the width of the fabric to be printed. The overall design of the cloth is built up by successive printings of the block, on which the design has been formulated so that it repeats. This is described in the section on repeating pattern (see page 23), but all this really means is that the pattern on the block must be arranged so that with each impression of the block, the pattern joins up on every side with the impressions which surround it, so creating a repeating pattern.

Registration of the block, the accurate placing of the block after each successive printing, alongside or above the previous print can be extremely difficult. Devices such as tiny pins attached to each corner of the printing side of the block, which create small holes, would help facilitate the registration but are rarely completely successful. Each repeat of the block is a separate operation where the dye has to be reapplied after each impression. This results in block-printed fabrics having a charm and character which, ironically, are more to do with the small imperfections inherent in the process than any deliberate planning.

DEVELOPMENT OF BLOCK PRINTING

Inevitably, in the search for a more efficient means of producing finer detailed prints and faster methods of production than are possible by hand, block printing as a mainstream form of production very quickly disappeared in favour of copperplate printing, initially from flat, hard, engraved metal plates. However, the real breakthrough came in 1783 when Thomas Bell, a Scot, invented a cylinder printing machine which allowed all types of designs to be reproduced in large quantities at very low prices.

After the invention of copperplate printing, block printing entered a new phase. Displaced by industrialization, the craft survived as a specialized form of printing, particularly on wallpaper and cloth. Notable exponents of hand-block printing were William Morris, G. and J. Baker and Liberty. The last two firms had almost stopped production by the early 1960s although hand-blocked wallpapers are still produced by a few firms today.

Elsewhere, block printing was developed as a rural craft producing relatively short runs of simple, but nevertheless extremely beautiful cloths. Two examples are the peasant cloths printed in parts of Czechoslovakia and American folk art cloths from New England.

To fully appreciate the special qualities of block printing, particularly early wooden block printing, spend a day in the textile study rooms in a museum such as the Victoria & Albert in London. You can gain much valuable information from studying early printed fabrics, in particular about the colouring and quality of the design, and the arrangement of the printing onto the cloth.

LINO BLOCK PRINTING

Linoleum, usually associated with floors, very quickly became established as an extremely efficient surface from which to cut blocks and its introduction ensured the continued use of block printing in a craft context. Linoleum, more usually known as its abbreviated form, lino, was the invention, thought to be accidental, of a Yorkshireman, Frederick Walton, who mixed ground cork with oxidized linseed oil; the mixture was then applied to a canvas backing. The name is derived from the Latin *linum* (flax) and *oleum* (oil).

Linoleum is easy to use and is a relatively inexpensive, waterproof material. It can be cut in any direction and is far easier to obtain than the specialist woods required for block cutting. The introduction of linoleum gave the craft of block printing new impetus. Starting in the 1930s a formidable collection of educationalists, designers, craftsmen and artists used linoleum, and among these were Enid Marx, Phyllis Barron and Edward Bawden.

PREPARING THE LINO BLOCK

Linoleum suitable for cutting and block printing can be purchased from most art suppliers. We used to buy rolls of old-fashioned brown lino and then cut off pieces as we required them. These rolls are increasingly hard to find and our previously reliable source of lino rolls now finds it easier to sell lino in 30 cm (12 in) squares. This is a good size for the methods we use. The lino is far more manageable if you mount it on a block of wood; this applies both to blocks to be used for individual prints on paper and for printing fabric. Lino mounted on a wooden block is much easier to handle than unmounted lino which is rather flexible. If you have bought 30 cm (12 in) squares of lino it is most convenient to mount the whole piece at one time and then cut it into the size required. Alternatively, cut the ready-mounted blocks to the size required as you need them. Materials such as plywood and blockboard of a thickness of approximately 12–20 mm (½–¾ in) provide an ideal support for lino.

To mount the lino, glue it to the block of wood with a waterproof glue, then place a heavy weight on top until the layers are firmly stuck together. Once dry, the lino block can be cut. Make sure that you cut your blocks accurately to the required size. This will be a great help later on when the blocks need to be accurately registered. Before you transfer the design to the block, place it face down on a sheet of sandpaper and gently rub the surface of the lino to remove any gloss coating and to help the ink or pigment adhere to the surface when printing. If any of the edges of the block are rough these should also be gently sanded. The block is now ready for use.

TRANSFERRING THE PATTERN ONTO THE BLOCK

We cannot stress enough the importance of accuracy when drawing or cutting your design, and also the importance of planning your

LINO-BLOCK PRINTED CURTAINS ECHO A MARITIME THEME IN THIS CORNER OF OUR HOUSE.

1 The block must first be prepared by gently sanding it to remove the shiny surface of the lino.

2 Carbon paper is laid face down onto the block. A tracing of the design is then laid on the carbon paper and the design transferred onto the block.

designs to the required width of the fabric. Fabric that is 90 cm (36 in) wide would require two repeats of 45 cm (18 in) square blocks, three repeats if the blocks were 30 cm (12 in) square, four repeats if they were 23 cm (9 in) square and six repeats if 15 cm (6 in) square and so on. It is important to do the job properly, not least because it is very annoying suddenly to find that your pattern and block are not exactly the same size. If they do not fit or join exactly the mistake will have a cumulative effect right through the printing process.

We suggest you start lino-block printing using small blocks of 7.5 cm (3 in) or 10 cm (4 in) squares until you are familiar with the technique. We also suggest that your first designs should be kept quite simple. We dis-

cuss design ideas and problems in Design Considerations (page 16).

If your design is very simple you can simply draw it straight onto the block with a pencil. If it is more complicated, take a tracing of the original design to the exact size of the block. Place a piece of carbon paper face down on the block, then put the tracing paper on top and draw over the design on the tracing paper. The drawing is then transferred onto the block by means of the carbon paper.

CUTTING THE BLOCK

Cutting into lino is not difficult. Lino-cutting tools, or gouges, are easily available and there are many variations in size and shape. We find that we use only about three sizes of gouge and a sharp knife shaped like a scalpel, so you may like to experiment with a few before buying a complete set. We find a V-shaped gouge useful for following the lines of the design, and a U-shaped gouge excellent for clearing the areas in between. The sharp point of the knife is useful for removing difficult corners and also for areas with very fine detail.

The lino may seem hard to cut sometimes, especially in cold weather. You can warm it gently in front of a fire but you will find it soon warms up naturally as you work into it. You will soon tell with experience how deep to cut but you must cut away enough lino to produce a clear impression of the part that you wish to print; background gouge marks may appear occasionally, do not worry about these as they give the print additional character.

Always cut into the block against a solid surface to avoid slipping. Never cut or gouge

towards your hand – always cut away from you and never leave your hand in the path of the gouge.

There are two very different ways of applying colour to the block depending on whether you are printing with dyestuff on fabric or with inks on paper.

LINO-BLOCK PRINTING ON FABRIC

This method of applying colour to the block is, in our experience, the most straightforward. We use pads to hold the dye and the principle is very similar to that of the ink pad used with rubber stamps.

MAKING A PAD FOR FABRIC PRINTING

Making an ink pad is very simple and an example is shown in the general photograph on block printing (see page 62–3). For the base of the pad choose a block of wood or board approximately the size of a fairly large book, say 23 x 25 cm (9 x 10 in). Over this stretch four or five layers of soft woollen blanket or similar soft material. Stretch this tightly and fix with upholstery nails around the edges of the block. Stretch PVC-covered cloth over this as tightly as possible and fasten as before on all sides of the pad. The pad is now waterproof and soft. Now stretch across the pad a soft felt cloth and attach on two sides using upholstery nails. This is the surface onto which you brush colour or dyestuff when printing. If you are printing more than one colour for your design you will need a pad for each colour.

PRINTING THE BLOCK

Paint the dyestuff onto the felt surface of the pad with a brush. Press the lino block onto the

3 *The lino surface is cut away to leave a clear outline of the element to be printed. The stop-block provides a rest against which to hold the lino block while cutting – which must always be away from the body.*

4 *The printing pad is brushed with dyestuff until an even layer is applied. The process is repeated after each printing of the block.*

5 *The block is gently dabbed onto the pad until the printing surface has an even layer of dyestuff on it.*

pad once or twice or until the print face of the block is charged with colour. Print the block onto prepared fabric which is stretched on the printing board. Repeat the process and brush more colour onto the pad as required at regular intervals. When the printing is finished the felt part of the pad must be removed and washed out. The dyestuff is not fixed at this stage and the felt can be used again and again. If you are leaving your printing for only a few hours you can cover the pad with a plastic bag to stop the dyestuff from drying out.

When you are actually printing the block and you have placed it carefully on the fabric you need to gently bang the back of the block with the end of the handle of a mallet to ensure even coverage of the dyestuff.

6 *The block is carefully positioned in place on the cloth and gently tapped on the back with a mallet to ensure an even distribution of the image.*

FLOWER BLOCKS

WE CHOSE THESE CURTAINS, LINO BLOCK-PRINTED WITH INKY-BLUE FLOWERS, FOR OUR STUDIO. THE ROOM HAS GLAZED TERRACOTTA WALLS, SO WE KEPT THE NATURAL COLOUR THEME AND PRINTED THE FLOWERS ONTO HEAVY UNBLEACHED CALICO. THE STUDIO'S PROPORTIONS ARE NOT SYMMETRICAL AND WE USED COMPLEMENTARY LINO CUTS FOR THE DIFFERENTLY SHAPED WINDOWS. LINO BLOCK-PRINTED FABRICS OFTEN SEEM TO GIVE INTERIORS A 1930S OR 1940S FEEL. WE CHOSE TO ENHANCE THIS EFFECT BY LETTING SOME THE BACKGROUND TO THE FLOWERS PRINT FAINTLY. YOU CAN SEE THIS PROCESS IN MORE DETAIL OVERLEAF. THE MOTIFS ARE QUITE LARGE, BUT WITH CAREFUL HANDLING CREATE A BOLD AND CONFIDENT EFFECT. IT IS ALSO INTERESTING TO SEE HOW A LARGE LENGTH OF FABRIC CAN EASILY BE PRINTED FROM A RELATIVELY SMALL PRINT PAD.

1 *The print pad is inked, and the prepared lino block is dabbed carefully onto the print pad until it has picked up an even layer of dyestuff.*

2 *The block is placed onto the fabric and the back gently tapped with the mallet to ensure an even printing. Note that we have carefully ironed in vertical folds so that they can be used as guidelines for the printing.*

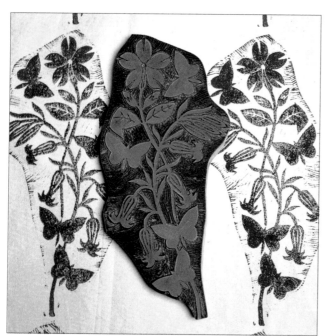

ABOVE AND RIGHT: THE TWO BLOCKS SHOWN WITH THE PRINTS THEY PRODUCE ON THE FABRIC. ALTHOUGH MUCH OF THE UNWANTED AREA HAS BEEN CUT AWAY, SOME OF THE BACKGROUND HAS STILL PRINTED. ALTHOUGH WE LIKE THE FEEL OF THIS, WE WILL PROBABLY CUT MORE OF THE BACKGROUND WITH A JIGSAW.

A FINISHED LENGTH OF
PRINTED FABRIC.

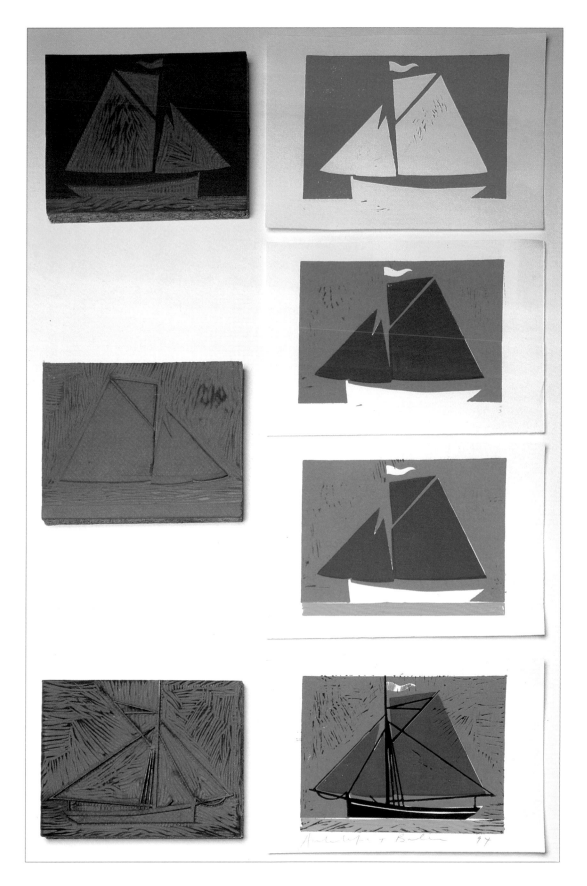

PROGESSIVE LINO BLOCKS WITH RESULTING PRINTS TAKEN FROM THEM, SHOWING HOW THE FINAL
IMAGE IS BUILT UP. THE CUT-AWAY BACKGROUND AREAS INEVITABLY RETAIN SOME INK WHICH WILL PRINT.
THIS IS VERY MUCH PART OF THE TECHNIQUE AND GIVES TEXTURE AND LIFE TO THE FINAL PRINT.

LINO-BLOCK PRINTING ON PAPER
Printing inks

Water-soluble printing inks in tubes are best for lino-block printing on paper. These inks are available from most art suppliers; they are extremely economical and easy to use. There are also oil-based waterproof inks easily available. They are used in the same way, but water-soluble inks are cleaned from equipment with water while oil-based inks are cleaned off using white spirit. (On a practical level cleaning equipment in water is a lot less messy than cleaning with white spirit). Both types of inks are available in good colour ranges which can be intermixed within the same type, and although water-soluble inks dry more quickly than oil-based inks the latter are considered to be more permanent. If you want to print a series of images consistency is important and it is best to stick to one type of ink and to use a reliable brand.

Old books on printing are a good source of information, such as this recipe for powder colour mixed with rice starch, useful for printing lino cuts onto large surfaces: prepare the rice starch by mixing 2 teaspoons of rice flour into boiling water and beating until the liquid thickens. Add this directly to the powder pigment. No other medium is necessary and you can now apply the colour directly to the

OUR FAVOURITE FLATFISH PRINT HAS BEEN PRINTED IN WATER-SOLUBLE INKS, AND HIS SPOTS DABBED IN WITH A SPONGE AFTER PRINTING.

printing block itself, using a hogshair brush.

Printing inks are far less fluid than most dyestuffs and require the use of a roller to apply the ink to the surface of the block.

Printing rollers, made from rubber or gelatine, are sold at most good craft shops. Printing inks sold in tubes are also easily available. We tend to use water-based inks because we prefer the quality and also because they are less messy and easier to clean up. You will need a good, flexible palette knife for mixing the inks and colours and also a sheet of strong, thick glass. The glass provides a good surface on which to mix the colour required and on which to spread the ink. Spread the ink using the roller until the roller is evenly coated with ink. Then roll it onto the surface of the block ensuring the colour covers all parts of the design. Once complete, the prints can be hung up or placed somewhere to dry undisturbed and the sheet of glass, roller and palette knife and block washed, dried and stored.

For printing our editions of prints, sometimes running into hundreds, we use a rather unorthodox method, which although sounding rather crude is very efficient. For multiple production, place the blocks onto the paper to be printed and gently turn over the block and the paper so that the paper is now on top of the block. The wet ink is usually sufficient to keep the paper in place but it is a good idea to give the surface a gentle rub with your hand to make absolutely sure. Then carefully rub the back of a large spoon over the paper attached to the block. If you do this in good light it is very easy to see which parts of the paper have been rubbed and which have not. When you are sure that the whole surface has been printed carefully remove the paper.

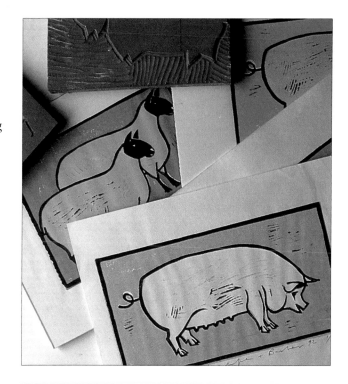

LEFT AND ABOVE: LINO-BLOCK PRINTS LIKE THESE ARE EXCELLENT FOR MAKING GREETINGS CARDS, GIFTS AND PRINTS TO HANG ON THE WALL. FOR ALL THESE FAMILIAR COUNTRYSIDE CREATURES WE HAVE WORKED TO SIMPLIFY THE FORMS UNTIL WE ARRIVED AT A STRONG GRAPHIC OUTLINE THAT WOULD BE EFFECTIVELY REINFORCED BY RELATIVELY LARGE AREAS OF FLAT COLOUR. OVERLEAF WE SHOW IN DETAIL HOW WE PRINTED OUR TWO BLACKFACE SHEEP IN A GREEN FIELD.

SHEEP PRINT

★

1 *The colours are mixed and rolled out onto a sheet of thick, strong glass. This has the double advantage of being smooth and easy to clean.*

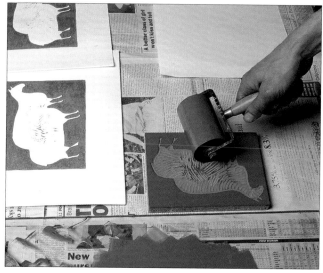

2 *With the roller, the first block is inked up. Since green is the largest area of colour, it is easier to start with – and provides a guide by which to keep the other colours in register.*

5 *The paper is peeled carefully off the block.*

6 *The next block delivers the grey of the sheep's bodies. It is inked and printed as before.*

3 The green block is carefully placed on the paper. The paper and block are equally carefully slipped to the edge of the table and turned over so that the paper is now on top of the block.

4 The back of the paper is gently rubbed with the back of the spoon to ensure an even transfer of ink.

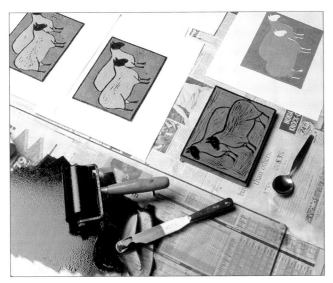

7 Finally, the block holding the outline of the sheep, and their black faces, is printed in black. This block also holds extra strokes and hatchings to give a lively surface to the print.

8 Mounted and framed, the print is now complete.

SILKSCREEN PRINTING

✳

*U*nlike some of the other methods of printing described, screen printing is a comparatively recent invention. This is surprising considering how closely related it is to ordinary stencilling which is a very old technique. Screen printing can be considered as a refinement of the stencilling process.

However skilled you are at cutting an intricate design into a piece of stencil paper, there is always the problem of bridging the floating parts of the stencil. This can be a very delicate operation. The central island of the letter O is a good example of a floating part. The solution to this problem is attributed to eighteenth-century Japanese printers. Their process involved cutting two identical stencils and sandwiching between the two a fine web of silk or human hair, glued with a varnish called *shibu* which secured the otherwise floating parts of the design. This style of printing, called *yuzen* required an exceptional degree of skill in its execution but it allowed designs to be produced which were otherwise virtually impossible to execute. Given the influence of the east in Europe in other areas of printing and textile development, it is strange that nothing more happened in the development of this process until 1907, when Samuel Simon of Manchester was granted a silkscreen process patent for the technique which influenced silkscreen printing as we know it today.

SILKSCREENED FABRICS AND PAPERS: SETTING UP FOR
A SILKSCREEN PRINTING TAKES TIME, BUT CAN TURN
OUT MULTIPLE IMAGES AT LARGER SIZES MORE
QUICKLY THAN POTATO PRINTING OR LINO BLOCK
PRINTING. HERE WE SHOW SOME OF OUR FAMILIAR
MOTIFS IN SCREEN-PRINTED FORM.

A basic screen consists of a rectangular frame usually made from wood but sometimes from metal. Over this screen a fine gauze, customarily silk bolting cloth or cotton organdie, is stretched as tightly as possible. Samuel Simon used a varnish-like substance which he painted onto a screen; when dry this prevented the dye or ink penetrating through the painted areas. The unpainted areas of the gauze allowed the free passage of the ink or dye. The screen was then placed on the surface to be printed, gauze side down. Ink or dye was brushed over the gauze as through a cut stencil, producing the image formed of cut and uncut areas.

The potential of silkscreen printing was quickly seen, particularly when in 1914 the Selectasine method was introduced in America. This method produced a multicoloured work from a single screen by progressively painting out the open areas on the screen once each colour had been printed. Instead of brushing the colour through the gauze, it was pushed through using a squeegee, a rubber blade with a handle that is pulled from one side of the screen to the other.

Many kinds of screen coatings were experimented with, everything from paper to wax crayon or varnish. Anything that would not dissolve or become detached in the printing medium was put into practice. It was, however, the advent of stencil films and photo-sensitive emulsions which allowed a vast range of reproduction possibilities in silkscreening, making it an extremely versatile technique. Stencil films can be cut very accurately using a fine blade, producing highly detailed designs; they can be chemically attached to the screen,

STENCILS PLAY AN IMPORTANT PART IN ALL OUR WORK, ALLOWING US TO CREATE BOLD PATTERNS AND MOTIFS. ON OUR TRADEMARK FLOWER PLATE, FOR EXAMPLE, WE USED A PAPER STENCIL TO MASH OUT THE FLOWER SHAPE. WE COULD EQUALLY HAVE USED THE SAME STENCIL TO CREATE A SCREEN PRINT OF A WHITE FLOWER AGAINST BLUE.

allowing for greater accuracy. Photo-sensitive emulsions coat the screen and are then exposed like a photograph, reproducing a vast range of images.

Silkscreening, though slow in getting started in relation to other techniques, quickly made the others obsolete in terms of serious production, particularly in the textile industry.

STENCILLING AS A PRINTING AID

Over the past few years there has been a huge revival of interest in the use of stencils as a technique for applying patterns, particularly to walls and furniture. Fine examples of stencilling in a domestic environment can be seen at the American Museum in Bath. In this book we are concerned with stencilling not as an end in itself, but as a means to an end. We use stencils as a tool to assist us in carrying out and repeating our designs.

An example of the way in which we use stencils is best shown in our ceramic design 'White Flower'. Here we use a flower shape cut out of stencil paper. This shape really only acts as a resist or barrier so that we can paint the cobalt blue over and around it. When the shape is removed the white flower is revealed, set against a blue background. Fine black lines and the centre detail are added by hand.

We will be showing you in this book how to cut paper stencils for use with our simple silkscreen process and they will crop up as an aid time and time again.

ABOVE RIGHT AND RIGHT: CUT PAPER STENCILS ARE AN ESSENTIAL TOOL IN SCREEN PRINTING, ALLOWING YOU TO REPEAT DESIGNS ACCURATELY AND IN REGISTER. IN THIS BOOK WE HAVE DELIBERATELY SHOWN THE SAME MOTIFS IN VARIOUS PRINTED FORMS. THE SHEEP AND BOAT SHAPES, FOR EXAMPLE, HAVE ALREADY BEEN SEEN AS LINO BLOCK PRINTS, BUT ARE EQUALLY EFFECTIVE AS THE BASIS FOR A SCREEN PRINT. PAGES 90–94 EXPLAIN THE PROCESS OF CUTTING A STENCIL AND PRINTING FROM IT IN STEP-BY-STEP DETAIL.

MAKING A SILKSCREEN FRAME

The screen used for silkscreen printing consists of a square or rectangular frame usually made from wood (but it can also be made of metal or plastic) inside which a fine gauze screen is stretched. We prefer to use wooden screens which can be purchased or made easily at home. If you decide to make your frame at home, bear in mind that you can also use an old picture frame, for example.

It is important to have good, strong frames that can be used over and over again, that will withstand the constant cleaning and washing without warping and will not fall apart. Marine

1 The fine gauze screen is attached to the wooden frame with a staple gun. Frames can be purchased ready made, or you can use an old picture frame, but note that the frame needs to be durable and non-warping.

ply can be used to make the frames but the best woods are soft woods – well seasoned – smooth woods such as red cedar, yellow pine, Kenya and other cedars. Use these in preference to hard woods. An ideal frame is prepared from pieces of timber roughly 4–5 cm (1½–2 in) deep and 6.5 cm (2½ in) wide. Thinner woods can be used, but it must be stressed that the sides of the screen must be strong because the gauze will be stretched very tightly across it. A strongly made screen will also last longer. Although screens can be very large, remember that if they are too large they are unmanageable. If you tailor the size of the screen to the width of a furnishing fabric you will have a screen that will print the full width of the fabric.

A screen used to print the full width of a furnishing fabric will be a long, large screen. When printing, you will need an assistant on either side of the printing table to hold each end of the screen and to pull the squeegee across its full width. The screen in this instance is long and narrow as the design has a narrow repeat. A large repeat would require a larger screen too awkward to handle.

When making a screen and deciding on the size required for the design you must remember to allow a margin of at least 5 cm (2 in) between the edge of the design and the inside of the screen on all sides and top and bottom. This is to provide an area for the dye to collect at each end after the squeegee has been pulled across, and also on the sides to allow the dye to pass freely, clear of the design, as it moves up and down the screen with the squeegee.

Finally, if you are making the screen yourself, it is a good idea to slightly round the outer edge of the wood of the frame to facilitate the stretching of the gauze over the edges and to prevent it tearing.

THE GAUZE SCREEN

The choice of gauze for the methods of screen printing described in this book is governed by cost and availability. Silk bolting, cotton organdie and nylon are all suitable for screen printing.

STRETCHING THE SCREEN

Stretching a screen is not difficult but it must be done carefully. While you can do it alone, it is far easier with someone to help you.

Cut the gauze slightly larger than the frame to allow it to be gripped and pulled firmly. Make sure that the warp and the weft of the gauze are running parallel to the sides of the frame. Use a staple gun to attach the gauze. To clarify this simple operation we will refer to each side of the frame as A, B, C and D running in a clockwise direction from the top.

Attach the gauze to A in the centre of the frame and then stretch and attach the gauze to side C in the centre, making sure that the warp in the gauze is straight.

Now stretch the gauze from side B to side D and staple in the centre, making sure that the weft is as straight as possible. Now work from A–C, from top to bottom, pulling the gauze as tightly as possible. When these edges are complete repeat from B–D. Take up any slack in the corners.

Technically the screen is now ready for use but for our purpose – a method where you use the same screen time and time again –

2 *Using gummed brown tape, seal off the margin between the printing area and the rest of the screen. It's necessary to do this on both sides of the gauze. When taping the inside, bring the tape well over the edges so there are no gaps.*

you now need to mask off the margin between the printing area and the rest of the screen. Mask this using gummed brown tape which you place on both sides of the screen and onto and over its corners. You then need to apply two or three coats of varnish. This masking produces a perfect, re-usable screen and reduces considerably the danger of the ink or dye slipping out around the sides during printing.

THE SQUEEGEE

The squeegee is essential to the screen printing

3 The brown paper strip must now be varnished top and bottom. Two or three coats should do. The aim is to produce a reusable screen that can be wiped down between printings. The varnished strips, too, provide a seal at the margin that prevents colour seeping through outside the printing area.

process. It consists of a long length of rubber inserted into a piece of wood and should be the full width of the screen, including the masked margin – this is most important. The rubber edge protrudes from the wood by approximately 4–5 cm (1½–2 in) and acts as a blade which is used to pull and push the dye across the screen so it is forced through the gauze into the paper or cloth being printed. To print, you place a line of dye or other printing medium into the masked margin at the end of the screen and then pull the dye across the surface of the screen with the squeegee. The number of times you do this depends on the dye being used and the surface of the cloth or paper being printed. To a certain extent this is a process of trial and error and will become easier after a little experimentation.

You may find it useful to drill a hole in either end of the handle of the squeegee and place either a 15 cm (6 in) nail or piece of dowelling in both ends so that the squeegee can be supported in an upright position if you need to leave it resting on the screen at any time, such as when replenishing the dye.

PRINTING WITH A SILKSCREEN

Silkscreen printing uses more dyestuff than the other methods we describe so make sure that you have enough before you start on a project. It uses much more dye because you need a large amount of dye on the end of the screen to start and because the technique allows for the printing of larger designs. The binder, the medium into which you mix the pigment, is not expensive but nevertheless you do not necessarily wish to waste it on experiments.

Two and a quarter litres (½ gallon) of binder will go a long way when printing with potatoes or lino blocks, not nearly as far when silkscreening. As a cheaper alternative we recommend ordinary household wallpaper paste mixed with a household dye, previously dissolved in cold water. You can mix buckets of it and experiment to your heart's delight. Use this paste only on papers; it is not suitable for fabric.

BLOCKING OUT THE SCREEN

In order to silkscreen an image you will need to make paper stencils to create a mask and to allow the dye or ink to appear only where you want it to. Our choice is white cartridge paper but you could try other papers such as tracing paper, newsprint, greaseproof and lining paper. Do not use proper stencil paper (oiled stencil paper) as it is much too thick to adhere to the screen.

Paper stencils are our choice for screen printing because they are not permanent. There are other substances that are semi-permanent that can be painted onto the screen and then removed. There are many ways of blocking out the parts of the screen that you do not want to print. These range from photosensitive emulsions, quick-drying varnishes and lacquers to hot painted wax. All these methods are worth experimenting with but they will not allow your screen gauze to be used again. They would also mean the added expense of a screen for each colour. In the case of a four-colour pattern, four screens would be needed. These considerations are not a problem for a professional studio where long runs of the same design are printed but they do present

problems in the context of this book where we are advocating maximum flexibility and simplicity.

All the work illustrated here has been printed with small screens and cut paper stencils. The screens can be used over and over again and for all types of designs. If you have between four and six screens ready stretched and available they will only need to be washed and dried between use. This is very helpful when experimenting with different ideas.

Silkscreening allows you to produce a variety of bold and colourful designs. Regardless of whether the design consists of a single motif or a repeated image, we recommend colouring it in or preferably cutting out each section in coloured paper. To explain this we have used as an example the blue jug with the pink tulips and green leaves on pages 90–1. As a practice run, take a tracing of the whole design, then lay the tracing over some red paper; place a sheet of carbon paper underneath and draw over the tracing of the tulip heads, leaving a duplicated drawing of tulip heads on the red paper. Cut these out and stick onto the original. Repeat the process for the leaves and the jug, using the appropriate coloured paper. This method of organizing the design gives a better indication of what the final version will look like, and also produces a coloured working design.

It is easy to check the design by placing the screen over the top. By looking through the screen you will be able to make sure that the design comfortably fits the printing area. If the design is too large or too small you can cut down or enlarge the cut-out elements.

CUTTING THE STENCILS

It is a good to cut two or even three sets of stencils for each colour. This to ensure that if anything goes wrong there are spares. It is useful to have spare stencils once you have started printing, and it is easier to cut them all at once rather than return to this initial stage when you are in the middle of printing.

Layer three sheets of white cartridge paper on top of each other, with a sheet of carbon paper on top, carbon-side down.

To cut the stencils, place a sheet of tracing paper over the final coloured design and trace over the image. Place the tracing over the sheets of white cartridge paper and draw over the design with a sharp pencil to make a carbon tracing. Repeat the process with fresh paper until you have traced all the parts of the image. Keeping the sheets together lay them on a piece of stiff card or a cutting mat and cut through with a stencil knife. The result will be nine sheets of paper each with three of the three elements that make up the design. The shapes that remain should be kept carefully as you may wish to use them as stencils to produce a negative of the image. This process is shown overleaf. They can also be used to mask out the printed areas in order to print a surround colour.

The use of positive and negative shapes is very interesting and we use it in our mixed techniques section as part of a project involving both block printing and silkscreen printing (see pages 132–5).

SECURING THE FABRIC

Before starting to print you will need to choose one of the following methods in order to secure the fabric, which has a tendency to slip during the process of squeezing the dye through the screen.

Method 1

Simply secure with masking tape onto the printing board. This is usually adequate.

Medod 2

Make a paste of gum arabic and water and boil for 10 minutes to produce a glue. Paint the glue lightly over the printing board. Iron the fabric onto the glued printing board. The glue will wash out later.

Method 3

Follow the same process as for Method 2 but stick down a backing cloth and then place the fabric to be printed on top securing the edges with pins. This is especially useful if you are using a flimsy fabric such as silk through which the dye could flood. The backing cloth provides a more absorbent surface. (Any of these methods can be used for attaching fabric while working with any of the other techniques in the book if the fabric is slipping or the dye flooding).

HERE THE SCREEN IS SHOWN INKED UP AND READY TO PRINT, WITH A PAPER STENCIL IN PLACE THAT WILL PRODUCE ELEMENTS OF OUR PENNSYLVANIA TULIP DESIGN SEEN TO THE RIGHT OF THE PICTURE. WE INCLUDED A JUG OF REAL TULIPS TO SHOW HOW NATURAL FORMS CAN INSPIRE DESIGNS. SIMPLIFIED INTO TWO DIMENSIONS THE JUG AND TULIPS BECOME A STRONG PATTERN ELEMENT, WHETHER USED IN ISOLATION ON A CUSHION COVER OR AS A REPEAT PATTERN ON A LARGER PIECE OF FABRIC (SEE PAGE 93).

1 Working with the jug and tulips image, we finally built up a master design constructed from coloured cut paper, which we carefully traced onto tracing paper.

2 Using carbon paper, we transferred the master image onto three pieces of white stencil card.

3 The master design was made up of three elements: the jug, the leaves and stalks, and the flowers. Each will be printed a different colour, therefore each will require its own stencil. Here we show the jug shape cut out of the card.

4 Here all three stencils have been cut out. You can see how the shapes removed from the card relate to the original cut-paper master design.

PREPARING THE PRINT

You will need to have three prepared screens to print the tulip image; alternatively, you can use one screen and wash and dry it between each colour application. Lay all the stencils out right side up and marked to show the top. Place a tracing of your image on the fabric (you could use the negative shapes) and position the design within the screen area. When satisfied take some measurements and mark each piece of fabric to be printed. For this image we marked the bottom of the jug and also the central vertical. This indicates where to place the screen in order to print the jug. Once the jug is printed all the other parts will fit into place.

As you are printing the jug first, place the jug stencil on the printing board and place the screen over it (the screen gauze is in contact with the stencil). Turn the stencil and the screen over together taking care to keep the image in position. Tape the stencil to the edges of the screen with masking tape and place in position on the cloth to be printed. Make sure that you have a bowl of warm water and kitchen towels to hand in order to keep your hands as clean as possible.

You are now ready to print.

5 The first stencil (the blue jug) is attached to the underside of the screen with masking tape.

6 Getting ready to print. Mixed to the right consistency, the pigment is spooned into the margin between the top of the screen and the print area. It would be ideal to have three screens prepared, one for each colour element. However, it is equally possible to print a run of one element. then remove the stencil from the screen, clean off the screen and start again with a new stencil and so on.

PRINTING YOUR DESIGN

Having mixed your binder and pigment to the required colour spoon it along the edge of the inside of the screen. With one hand holding the screen firmly in place and the other gripping the squeegee, pull the squeegee firmly across the screen. Once you have made sure that there is enough dye at the other end (pushed there by the movement of the squeegee), pull it back again firmly.

Gently remove the screen and prop it up at an angle so that the face of the screen is not touching anything. Remove the printed cloth from the printing board. Repeat the process as often as required carefully removing the cloths to dry. At least 12–24 images can be printed before the stencil paper gets too wet and saturated with dye for use.

Once you have printed all the blue jugs scrape off any excess dye from the squeegee and the screen and save it. If you are using only one screen, wash and dry this carefully before printing again. Otherwise only the squeegee will need to be cleaned. Repeat the process, printing each of the other colours in turn.

After each printing session wash the screens very thoroughly with a stiff washing-up brush. Finally iron the printed cloth to fix the dye according to the the manufacturer's instructions.

7 The pigment is spread evenly with the squeegee. One stroke towards you and one away should be sufficient.

8 You can see clearly here how the three stencils build up to create the finished design. To ensure that the elements fit together in the final print you will need to mark the back of the fabric with some location points – we used the base of the jug and the central vertical. Once the jug is in position, all the other parts will fit into place.

OPPOSITE: A DETAIL FROM A 4-METRE LENGTH
OF CURTAIN FABRIC SCREEN-PRINTED
WITH THE PENNSYLVANIA TULIP MOTIF.

LEFT: A STRONG, CLEAN LOOK CAN BE ACHIEVED BY SILK-SCREENING AND WE HAVE CAPITALIZED ON THIS BY USING BRIGHT COLOURS AND SIMPLE SHAPES. HERE, OUR PENNSYLVANIA TULIP DESIGN IS PRINTED ONTO HEAVY COTTON SHEETING.

ABOVE: WE ORIGINALLY SCREEN PRINTED THE DUCK MATERIAL TO USE AS A BED COVER, BUT IT LOOKED MORE FUN AS A WALL-HANGING. THE SAME STENCIL WAS USED TO PRINT THE PILLOWCASES AND ALSO TO CREATE THE FRAMED PRINT. SCREEN PRINTING IS A VERY PRACTICAL WAY TO PRODUCE LARGE PIECES.

IN THIS VARIATION, A COT COVER HAS BEEN
PRINTED USING POSITIVE AND NEGATIVE STENCILS.
THE POSITIVE STENCILS ARE AGAINST THE NATURAL
COLOUR OF THE FABRIC, WHILE THE NEGATIVE
STENCIL REVERSES THE HORSE OUT AGAINST
A COLOURED BACKGROUND, LEAVING THE BODY OF
THE HORSE THE COLOUR OF THE FABRIC.
THE DAPPLED SPOTS WERE SPONGED IN AFTER
SCREEN PRINTING. A STENCILLED HORSE FRIEZE AND
A FRAMED SCREEN PRINT OF THE SAME SUBJECT
COMPLETE A THEMED EFFECT FROM THE REPETITION
OF A SINGLE MOTIF.

96

LEFT AND ABOVE: THE SAME SCREEN-PRINTED BOAT MOTIF CAN BE USED
TO PROJECT VERY DIFFERENT CHARACTERS. TEAMED WITH STYLIZED SEAGULLS, FISH AND
SEAWEED, IT OFFERS A SUITABLY JAUNTY MARITIME AIR WHEN MADE UP
AS A BOAT CUSHION. UNADORNED AS A DUVET COVER AND WALL PRINT IT PRODUCES,
ON THE CONTRARY, A RATHER COOL, SOPHISTICATED 'LOOK'.

A silkscreened chequerboard effect with ducks and cockerels for our kitchen. The overall design consists of positive and negative shapes in bright primary colours – a white duck on a blue background and a blue cockerel on a white background. The screen consisted of two negative duck stencils and two blank stencils arranged so as to print the blue and white grid first. Another screen was used to print the cockerel and two more screens (red and yellow) to print details.

ABOVE: THE CAFE CURTAIN WAS DESIGNED TO HIDE
AN UNSIGHTLY RETAINING WALL AND BRING
SOME COLOUR TO A RATHER GLOOMY CORNER.

LEFT: A STRIP LEFT OVER FROM
THE CAFE CURTAIN IS FUN AS A TRADITIONAL-STYLE
SHELF DECORATION.

RESIST
PRINTING &
DYEING

✳

$\mathcal{S}$o far we have dealt in detail with printing
techniques in which the colour is applied
directly to the printed surface. The technique
of dyeing cloth so as to leave a motif reversed
out in negative was first developed to the high-
est degree in India. Printed Indian cloths introduced into Europe from 1600 were the result
of as many as eleven stages of manufacture, all
by hand. These cloths inspired the European
textile industry to develop its own fabric printing methods. Resist dyeing is a basic approach
which is relatively easy to learn.

Four processes are involved in resist printing and dyeing although it is in fact a single
technique. These processes are: preparing the
resist, the application of the resist, the dyeing
of the cloth and finally the removal of the
resist. The whole process is best explained in
terms of drawing onto a sheet of plain white
paper with a candle or a wax crayon and
applying water colour with a large, flat brush
over the complete surface. Where the wax has
been applied it will resist the paint, leaving
those areas white. The same principle can be
applied to cloth using hot wax or other type of
resist applied with a block. The cloth is then
immersed in a cold dye bath.

A RICH SELECTION OF INDIGO WAX AND PASTE
RESISTS, TOGETHER WITH SOME OF THE WOODEN
BLOCKS USED TO PRINT THEM. NOTE THAT THE
BLOCKS USED TO PRINT THE RESISTS ARE ENTIRELY
DIFFERENT TO THE LINO BLOCKS DESCRIBED EARLIER
IN THE BOOK.

RESIST PRINTING

We use two methods of resist printing. The first is wax resist, the second is a cold paste resist. Lino blocks can be used with the cold paste resist, but are not suitable for wax printing as the hot wax would eventually destroy the lino eventually dislodging it from the block. For this reason we use wooden blocks to apply wax resist. It is possible to achieve fine work by cutting intricately detailed patterns into wooden blocks but this is specialist work and outside the scope of this book. Instead we cut wooden blocks into bold shapes which, when printed with a hot wax resist, leave strong areas of white, which when dyed stand out. We then use lino-block printing to fill these areas, giving the detail required to complete the wax resist design. The process is explained in the section on mixed techniques beginning on page 122.

PREPARING THE BLOCK FOR WAX RESIST PRINTING

To use the wooden blocks, take a strip of standard timber 5 x 2.5 cm (2 x 1 in) and place the edge in hot wax. This produces a very good resist stripe. Similarly, you could use a square piece of square wood to produce a check. To make blocks to your own designs it is useful to use a modern hand-held jigsaw with thin blades which are capable of cutting almost any shape very easily. This calls for very basic carpentry skills. We cut our shapes, mostly birds, animals and flowers this way. Try to keep images to be used for wax-resist printing simple and uncomplicated. As you will need to hold these blocks in the hot wax you will need to make a handle out of a long screw which is screwed into the back of the wooden block. This prevents your fingers from getting burnt as you lift the block in and out of the hot wax.

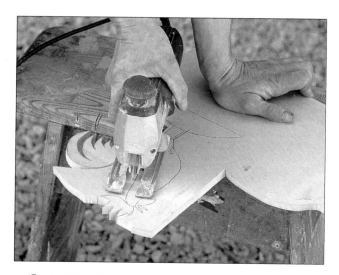

CUTTING A BLOCK, OR PROFILE, OF A COCKEREL OUT OF MDF BOARD WITH A HAND-HELD JIGSAW. THE MOTIF CAN BE HAND DRAWN ONTO THE BOARD, OR A TRACING CAN BE TRANSFERRED ONTO THE BOARD USING THE CARBON PAPER METHOD DESCRIBED EARLIER IN THE BOOK.

A COLLECTION OF MDF PROFILES USED FOR RESIST PRINTING. THE SHEEP AND HORSE ARE FAMILIAR MOTIFS FROM OUR FARM ANIMAL SERIES.

PREPARING THE WAX

Wax for printing can be paraffin wax or beeswax or a mixture of the two. The types are easily identifiable: paraffin wax is nearly always white and beeswax is honey-coloured. Paraffin wax is the wax normally used for making candles. Pure paraffin wax produces a harder, more brittle resist than beeswax but these properties are more applicable to wax painting or batik where the ability of the wax to produce cracks and fine lines, once hardened onto the cloth, gives batik its characteristic vein-like appearance. You can buy wax from craft shops, and this is usually a mixture of paraffin wax and beeswax. We often melt down ordinary household candles to obtain our paraffin wax.

Hot wax can be extremely dangerous unless handled with caution and common sense. Always use a bain marie or double boiler with a thermometer. Never put the wax to melt in a pan directly on the naked flame. You can buy special wax heaters from specialist craft shops and there are many electric domestic appliances on the market with a built-in thermostat (frying pans and chip pans, for instance). These are much safer and keep the wax at the correct temperature. Keep the appliance or bain marie for wax only. Whichever method you choose to melt the wax always have a fire blanket to hand. The temperature of the wax should be maintained between 55°C (130°F) and 60°C (140°F) or very slightly hotter if needed. The hot wax is dangerous much above this temperature. We repeat, no naked flame must go near the pan containing the wax. The hot wax will start to smoke and smell above 60°C (140°F).

THE EQUIPMENT NEEDED FOR PRINTING HOT WAX IS VERY SIMPLE. (TOP LEFT) PROPRIETARY WAX HEATER WITH ADJUSTABLE TEMPERATURE CONTROL AND AN OVEN THERMOMETER. (LEFT) WAX GRANULES, AVAILABLE FROM ART SUPPLIES SHOPS. (CENTRE) FIRE BLANKET AND FIREPROOF GLOVE. HOT WAX CAN BE VERY DANGEROUS UNLESS HANDLED WITH CAUTION: TEMPERATURE SHOULD NOT RISE MUCH ABOVE 60°C (140°F), AND NO NAKED FLAME SHOULD BE ALLOWED NEAR IT. IF THE WAX STARTS TO SMOKE AND SMELL, TURN OFF THE HEAT. AT ALL TIMES, IF IN DOUBT, TURN OFF THE HEAT AND COVER THE HEATER CAREFULLY WITH THE FIRE BLANKET.

PRINTING THE WAX

While the other techniques described in this book can be fitted in between other activities or in an evening, both resist printing and dyeing require a day or afternoon set aside for the purpose. Both activities are enjoyable and it is a good idea to have a session, resist printing lots of lengths and trying out lots of ideas. Then, at a later date, have a dyeing session. This is particularly relevant if using an indigo vat as it takes time to prepare the dye; also, as the indigo vat is used up or the colour becomes exhausted the vat produces lovely shades of pale blue and you need time to get to this stage. We deal with dyeing in more detail in the next chapter (page 112).

To print the wax onto fabric, use a wooden board kept solely for the purpose. Ideally the board should be approximately the same size as the printing board. After printing, the hard wax can be scraped off the wooden board and re-used. Alternatively, cover the board with cloth and sprinkle with china clay or fine sand, which will help prevent the hot wax printed cloth from sticking to the board. Keep the heated wax as near as possible to the printing board so that it does not lose too much heat as you work and also to ensure that you can print the wax as quickly as possible.

To print, heat the cold printing block up in the hot wax. When the wax is at the correct temperature lift the wood block out by the handle. Allow any drips to fall back into the pan, and then place the block very quickly and carefully in position on the cloth. Very little pressure is required and we recommend a couple of test runs on some old fabric to familiarize yourself with the technique. When you have finished printing set the fabric aside to await dyeing. Handle with care as the wax will peel off if crushed.

 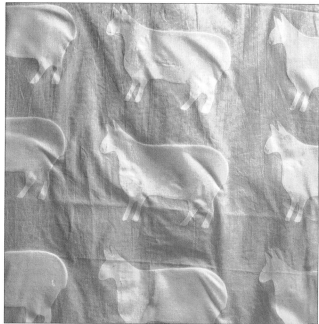

PRINTING THE WAX ONTO THE FABRIC.
ABOVE LEFT: THE WOOD BLOCK HAS BEEN HEATED UP IN THE HOT WAX, REMOVED, LETTING THE DRIPS FALL
BACK IN THE PAN, THEN PRINTED WITH LIGHT PRESSURE ONTO THE FABRIC.
ABOVE RIGHT: THE DRIED WAX RESISTS.

THE PRINTED FABRIC.
ONCE THE RESISTS
ARE WASHED OUT OF
THE DYED FABRIC,
THE SHEEP APPEAR
REVERSED OUT OF
THE BACKGROUND
COLOUR. THEY CAN BE
LEFT THE NATURAL
COLOUR OF THE
FABRIC, BUT WE OFTEN
OVERPRINT THE SHAPES
WITH AN OPAQUE
WHITE PIGMENT, USING
THE SAME
WOODEN PROFILE.

PASTE RESIST

We use the following recipe for our cold water resist paste: mix together 100 g (2 oz) plain flour and 100 ml (4 fl oz) cold water and bring to the boil. Boil until the paste is glutinous. Set aside while you make another paste from 100 g (4 oz) acacia and 100 ml (4 fl oz) water, and boil this until glutinous. Mix the two pastes together and then dilute with 250–500 cc boiling water, boiling for approximately 1 hour, stirring occasionally. This is the resist paste, it is best applied warm (hand hot) as it gets very sticky when it goes cold!

Printing with a paste is a less frenetic and a gentler process than printing with wax. Paste resists are applied in exactly the same way as lino blocks are printed, that is from printing pads. While it is possible to use the same pads that you use for dye simply by changing the felt, it is better to have separate pads for the paste. Place the wooden or lino block to be printed on the pad and print in the same way as for pigment printing (see page 68, lino block printing). Allow the paste to dry thoroughly on the fabric before handling. Handle the cloth very carefully before dyeing as the paste will peel off if the fabric is treated roughly. The paste-resisted cloth can now be dyed in a cold water dye or indigo vat (see pages 112–116).

There are no hard and fast rules, but it is generally better to use paste resists with indigo rather than modern cold-water dyes, which are much stronger. If redipping in either type of dye, you may need more than one application of the resist. It can also be a good idea to print both sides of the fabric. As always, we recommend that you experiment to find out what works.

ABOVE: POT OF PASTE RESIST, PRINTING PAD WITH HORSE PROFILE PLUS OTHER WOODEN PROFILES OF FAMILIAR MOTIFS. BELOW: THE PRINT PAD IS PAINTED WITH THE PASTE RESIST, ALREADY ONE HORSE HAS BEEN PRINTED IN PASTE ONTO THE FABRIC.

The fabric printed with the horse paste resist.

ABOVE: BUILDING UP THE HORSE PATTERN.
BELOW: OUR SEAGULL PATTERN
RESIST-PRINTED CLOTH HANGING OUT TO DRY
BEFORE BEING FURTHER OVER-PRINTED WITH
A LINO BLOCK (SEE OPPOSITE).

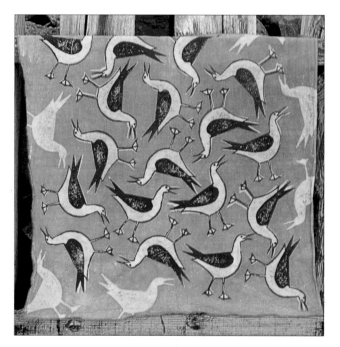

REMOVAL OF THE RESIST

After resist printing your fabric with wax or paste and then dyeing it using either indigo or with a cold-water dye, you will need to remove the wax or paste resist after dyeing. The two processes are as follows:

1 To remove the paste resist, repeatedly wash the fabric by hand in hot, soapy water. The paste will dissolve when wet.

2 The removal of the wax is achieved by several means. If you have a thick layer of wax scrape some off before doing anything else. Then boil the cloth, not too vigorously, in a solution of detergent and borax (1 tablespoon of borax to a bucket of water). This removes most of the wax from the cloth. Wash the cloth again and dry. If there is still a residue of wax remove it by ironing the cloth between sheets of newsprint or other absorbent paper. (Do not use newspaper or the ink may mark the fabric.) The wax will be absorbed by the paper. Keep moving the paper as it becomes saturated. Traces of wax may be left in the cloth and this gives a particular whiteness to the fabric. When the resist has been removed, the fabric is ready for use.

RIGHT:
THIS SEAGULL FABRIC HAS BEEN PRINTED USING
OUR PASTE RESIST DYED WITH INDIGO, BUT USING
A SLIGHTLY WEAKER VAT THAN WE USED TO PRINT
THE SHEEP FABRIC. INTERESTINGLY, THE PASTE
PRODUCES A SOFTER, MORE DELICATE QUALITY
THAN WAX. THIS EXAMPLE SHOWS WHERE THE
RESISTED AREAS HAVE BEEN PRINTED INTO USING
A LINO BLOCK TO GIVE OUTLINE AND DETAIL.

DYEING

DYEING FABRIC

There is no single, universal method of dyeing because there are many different types of dyestuff; these have been developed to deal with a very wide range of natural and synthetic fabrics. In this book we deal with two types only – indigo and Procion. These two types could hardly be more different: indigo is an ancient dyestuff, whereas Procion dyes were first developed in 1955. Indigo is termed a 'vat dyestuff': it has first to be combined with a chemical before the colour can penetrate the fibres of the cloth. Procion dyes are termed 'reactive dyes', meaning that the colour is fixed to the fibres of the cloth by chemical bonding.

Finally, indigo dyes in one colour range only – blue – while Procion dyes are available in a good range of colours.

INDIGO DYEING

Traditionally, indigo is derived from the *Indigofera tinctoria* plant. Although natural indigo is still available, most indigo dyes are now synthetic. A German chemist, Dr Alfred Bayer, discovered in 1897 that indigo could be produced chemically from coal tar. Synthetic indigo is easily obtained from most specialist art suppliers in the form of granules. Our recipe specifies granules – the other types of synthetic indigo require rather different methods.

Along with the granules, you will need sodium hydrosulphate (available from the same suppliers) which is the essential ingredient for

preparing the indigo vat. Although the word 'vat' has now come to mean 'vessel', it properly refers to the process of combining, or 'vatting', the indigo with the sodium hydrosulphate. Finally, you will need a quantity of caustic soda (sodium hydroxide).

From this list of ingredients you will guess that the chemistry of indigo dyeing is quite complex. Essentially the indigo and sodium hydrosulphate are combined with water in a dyebath to produce a weak organic acid, which is then neutralized with caustic soda to form a water-soluble salt. This salt has an affinity with natural fibres, for example wool, cotton and silk.

Strangely enough, the resultant liquid in the vat is not blue but bright yellow. Fabric gently dipped into the bath easily absorbs the yellow dye. It must then be carefully spread out without any parts being allowed to overlap, and hung from a washing line to become an even blue colour. This colour change happens during the process of oxidation which takes place as the dyed fabric is exposed to the air.

Different depths of blue are achieved by successive dippings between which the fabric is allowed to hang. Care should be taken when re-dipping the fabric as the reverse process happens as it re-enters the dye vat – if too many air bubbles enter the vat with the fabric, the vat contents will start to turn blue and the process will not work.

Preparing the vat

Choose a warm day for indigo dyeing as the vat must not get too cold. To use the vat on a cold day, tie lots of old newspapers around it to provide some insulation. Place the vat on several layers of newspaper. We tend to make an indigo vat every 3 to 4 months and dye all our prepared cloth at once, however a small vat can be made easily by reducing the quantities in the following recipe proportionately.

The recipe

54 litres (12 gallons) warm water (20–25°C/ 68–77°F)

1 kg (2.2 lb) of sodium chloride (common salt)

50 g (2 oz) caustic soda previously dissolved in 1 litre (1.1 pints) cold water

170 g (6 oz) sodium hydrosulphate (sodium diothionite)

250 g (8½ oz) synthetic indigo grains

ABOVE: A DETAIL OF OUR INDIGO-DYED FABRIC.

ABOVE LEFT: EQUIPMENT FOR INDIGO DYEING. NORMAL HOUSEHOLD UTENSILS CAN BE USED – A PLASTIC BUCKET WOULD DO FOR OUR RATHER SMART STAINLESS STEEL PAIL, FOR EXAMPLE – BUT REMEMBER TO KEEP ALL EQUIPMENT LOCKED AWAY FROM KITCHEN AREAS AND CHILDREN.

Heat the water to the required temperature, add the sodium chloride and stir with a wooden stick until dissolved. Add the caustic soda solution and stir gently. Gently sprinkle the sodium hydrosulphate onto the surface of the liquid, and then stir in the indigo grains.

Stir extremely gently to avoid any air bubbles getting into the vat.

Keep air out of the vat as much as possible at all times and cover with a closely fitting lid when not in use.

The process

The fabric, unless paste-resisted, will have been soaked to await dyeing. Make sure that you are wearing rubber gloves and lower the fabric, keeping it as flat as possible, into the vat without making any bubbles and leave for approximately 1½ minutes. Both the contents

of the vat and the cloth will be bright yellow.

Remove the cloth extremely carefully and hang to allow oxidation to take place. Do not let any folds or creases appear as these will stop the air from reaching all areas and will result in patchiness. The cloth will gradually change from yellow to blue.

Dip the cloth again for one minute and hang it up to re-oxidize. The longer it hangs in the air the better, but after an hour or so it can be rinsed in cold water to remove any surplus dye. The process is now complete. If you require a stronger blue than that achieved after the second dipping, repeat the dipping and hanging processes until you have the desired shade.

As you continue to use the vat its contents become exhausted and the strength of colour will be progressively weaker.

1 Adding the indigo grains to the water, sodium chloride and caustic soda solution. The indigo must be stirred in very gently to avoid beating air into the vat. We use a large heavy-duty plastic dustbin to make the indigo vat. The closely fitting lid, although not airtight, is handy for keeping the air out of the solution.

2 The length of cloth to be dyed is entered carefully into the vat. Again, the trick is to avoid trapping bubbles of air in the wet cloth which might get into the vat.

3 In a vat this size, lengths of 3 or 4 metres can be safely entered and left to soak.

4 The fabric is removed from the vat very slowly. As it is removed the colour changes immediately from the yellow of the vat to green.

5 As the fabric is hung out on the line, emerging blue areas can be seen as the fabric oxidizes and changes from yellow to green to blue.

6 Now the fabric must be hung from the line as flat as possible.

7 *After a short period hanging on the line the fabric can be redipped – several times, in fact, if an extremely dark blue is required.*

8 *A further dipping intensifies the colour.*

9 *Now the dyeing process is complete, the fabric hangs out to dry on the washing line, oxidizing to the final intended shade of blue.*

ABOVE: A SELECTION OF OUR INDIGO RESIST FABRICS ORIGINALLY DEVELOPED BY US IN OUR STUDIOS,
BUT SUBSEQUENTLY PRODUCED FROM OUR BLOCKS BY FACTORIES SMALL AND LARGE ELSEWHERE.
AS PRINTING WITH WAX IS A TRADITIONAL MALAYSIAN TECHNIQUE, IT WAS NICE TO HAVE OUR FISH DESIGN
MANUFACTURED FOR US IN MALAYSIA.

PROCION DYES AND DYEING

From the range of Procion dyes available you will need to specify Procion M, or Procion MX as it has more recently become known.

Unlike indigo dyeing, Procion dyeing is comparatively straightforward, and although it is unnecessary to give a detailed description of the process involved here, some points are worth noting. Procion dyes are particularly effective on mercerized cottons, and viscose rayon (both natural fibres) where it is possible to obtain good dark shades. Procion dyes also perform well on ordinary cotton, but to obtain these darker shades the cloth must be dipped repeatedly into the dye until the desired shade is reached. Procion dyes can be used to dye linen, silk and wool, and a wide range of colours is available. Procion dyes are fast when washed and when exposed to strong light. However, once the Procion dyebath has been prepared it is only suitable for use for 2–3 hours. It is important, therefore, that you plan the dyeing operation carefully because even though the dyebath may look no different it will not work after the three-hour time limit has expired.

Dyeing with Procion MX dyes in cold water

The recipe
25 g (1 oz) urea
300 ml (10 fl oz) boiling water
50 g (2 oz) Procion MX dyestuff
1 litre (1.1 pints) cold water
4 g (⅛ oz) soda ash (hydrous sodium carbonate)
8 g (¼ oz) sodium bicarbonate

ABOVE: EQUIPMENT FOR PROCION DYEING ARRANGED AND READY ON A TABLE. ALTHOUGH THE DYE MIXTURE IS NOT PARTICULARLY DANGEROUS, IT IS ALWAYS SAFE TO USE RUBBER GLOVES WHEN HANDLING CHEMICALS, AND TO KEEP ALL EQUIPMENT LOCKED AWAY FROM KITCHEN AREAS AND CHILDREN.

The process
Cloth to be dyed should primarily be pre-soaked. However, do not pre-soak the cloth before dyeing if it has been paste resisted. Pre-soak it only if you have used a wax resist or if you are over-dyeing a fabric already printed with pigment dyestuff or similar, having first fixed the pigment by ironing.

Dissolve the urea in the boiling water in a bucket. Leave the solution to cool to a temperature of 60°C (140°F). Put the Procion dye into a dustbin large enough to allow the fabric to move freely. Stirring continuously, slowly add the urea solution to the dyestuff. Then add 900 ml (4 fl oz) of the cold water to the dye solution.

In a separate bucket, prepare the alkali solution. Mix the soda ash and the sodium bicarbonate together and add the remaining 100 ml (4 fl oz) of cold water. Stir until dissolved.

When you are ready to dye your cloth, stir the alkali solution into the Procion dyebath. You will need to work fairly quickly since, as mentioned above, the dyestuff will not be effective for longer than about three hours, after which time it should be discarded.

Wearing rubber gloves, use your hands to agitate the fabric from time to time. After it has been in the dyebath for approximately 30 minutes, lift it out and hang out to dry. The dye will fix in the air taking about 24 hours. Allow a little longer if the air is cold, and less if it is warm. When the dye is fixed rinse the fabric to remove the excess dye. The process is now complete.

By this stage you will have realized that dyeing cloth, although in itself a relatively simple operation, involves some rather complicated chemical reactions. Much of this is for fixing the colour onto or into the cloth, to prevent the colour washing out or fading. In both indigo and procion dyeing this takes place both inside the dyebath and immediately after the fabric has been removed from it. The dyebath itself creates the conditions in which the fixing is achieved.

1 Procion dyeing is a fairly straightforward operation. Here the white wax resist fabric is entered into the dye bath.

2 A second piece of fabric is entered.

3 *The fabric is left to soak for approximately 30 minutes. From time to time the fabric should be agitated by hand.*

4 *Taking out the dyed fabric out of the bath. After drying in the air for about 24 hours, the fabric will need to be rinsed in water to remove excess dye.*

RIGHT:
DETAIL OF THE DUCK WAX-RESIST
FABRIC SHOWING HOW THE CRINKLING
OF THE WAX PRODUCES
A VERY INTERESTING VEINED,
ALMOST MARBLED EFFECT.

MIXED TECHNIQUES

✳

*I*n our introduction we have explained the general principle by which many extremely interesting results can be achieved by combining different techniques. However, in order to do this successfully we do stress the importance of thoroughly exploring all the methods we describe in order to appreciate their virtues and limitations; only then will the advantages of using one or other technique for a particular project become apparent and once the general concept has been understood not only are a great many possibilities opened up, but also a vast area of further experimentation. There are two areas here which we should clarify. In the first you use different techniques to produce the same or a complementary pattern or motif. This is particularly useful if a change of scale is required. The choice depending on which technique is most suitable for the design and for the surface to be printed.

In the second the pattern itself is composed of different techniques to produce an effect not possible by the use of one technique, or the execution of the pattern is made easier by using more than one technique.

MANY OF OUR INDIGO RESIST FABRICS ARE EXTREMELY GOOD EXAMPLES OF MIXING TWO OR MORE PRINTING TECHNIQUES. HERE THE FLOWERS HAVE BEEN RESIST PRINTED AND THE COLOURS INSERTED WITH LINO BLOCKS.

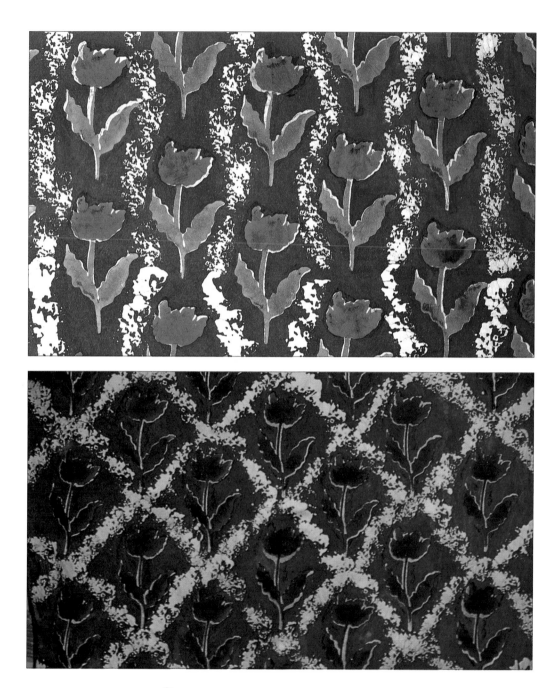

DAFFODIL AND TULIP BREAKFAST ROOM

THE WAX-RESISTED, INDIGO-DYED CLOTHS USED IN OUR BREAKFAST ROOM CREATE A VERY LIVELY EFFECT.
THE INDIGO IS VERY COLOURFAST AND WEARS AND AGES WELL. THE SPONGED-EFFECT VERTICAL STRIPES
WERE ACHIEVED BY PRINTING HOT WAX WITH A SPONGE. THIS IS EXTREMELY TRICKY AND YOU MUST MOUNT
THE SPONGE ON A SUPPORT IN ORDER NOT TO BURN YOURSELF.

THE DAFFODIL AND TULIP MOTIFS WERE PRINTED IN WAX RESIST USING WOODEN PROFILES. WE DYED
THE WAX-RESISTED CLOTH IN INDIGO SO AS TO ACHIEVE A MID-BLUE, BUT WE COULD HAVE CONTINUED TO
DIP THE CLOTH TO ACHIEVE A DARKER BLUE IF REQUIRED. THE COLOURS OF THE FLOWERS WERE APPLIED
USING LINO BLOCKS WITH PIGMENT DYESTUFFS, 'FIXED' ONTO THE FABRIC ACCORDING TO THE METHOD
DESCRIBED ON PAGE 43.

We use this method to produce many of our fabrics and in some cases, such as the seagull, a lino block has been used in conjunction with a wooden profile of the seagull, in others, such as the flowers, colour has been applied using a silkscreen in addition to the lino block which emphasizes the line or detail. A variation of the resist technique can also be used. This is to dye the cloth a solid colour and then print onto it with an opaque white pigment to achieve results similar to those achieved when using a resist. (Most manufacturers of pigment dyes produce an opaque white which will do this.) Potato printing has an advantage over the other techniques in that it is quick and simple and also relatively complex designs can be composed using more tints and colours than are possible with lino or silkscreen printing. A disadvantage is that the printing of large areas of pattern or colour are not possible. Mixed methods are especially useful here. An example is our jug of flowers. The flowers are potato printed and the jug produced from a paper stencil and silkscreened.

Another example of where a potato print is particularly useful is where a small area of colour is required such as in our print edition of a French fishing boat. Here the predominant technique used is lino blocks, one being used for each of the four colours. The tiny flag used a further two colours but in such insignificant amounts that it would not be worth cutting two further lino blocks. We solved this by using a potato cut as the flag and we brushed the colour in place and printed. Using potatoes to print lots of colours together, with a detailed one coloured lino block, is rather like the idea of hand colouring etchings and gives plenty of

scope if a lot of colours are required.

Another possibility is to use lino blocks and screen printing together. Screen printing can be used in a similar way to potato printing but on a much larger scale. Screen printing (as described in this book) lends itself to producing simple bold designs in flat strong areas of colour. Therefore it is ideal used in conjunction with lino block printing – the lino print in this case producing the detail.

We show this combination in our antelope prints. Positive and negative stencils have been used to produce areas which have been over-printed with the animals in black with lino blocks. There are many ways of combining the techniques and mixing the methods giving endless possibilities.

THE PURPOSE OF ALL FABRIC DESIGN IS TO BRING LIFE AND COLOUR TO A TWO-DIMENSIONAL SURFACE. IN FABRICS SUCH AS THIS WE COMBINE A NUMBER OF TECHNIQUES IN ORDER TO ACHIEVE THIS. THESE WILD ANIMALS, TUMBLED AROUND THE FABRIC IN A FASHION REMINISCENT OF CAVE PAINTINGS, ARE ALL SHOWN IN MOTION. THE BASIC SHAPES CAN BE RESIST DYED SO THAT THEY REVERSE OUT OF THE BACKGROUND COLOUR, OR THEY CAN BE LINO-BLOCK PRINTED WITH AN OPAQUE WHITE PIGMENT ON TOP OF A SOLID COLOUR. ON TOP OF THE SHAPES WE HAVE LINO-BLOCK PRINTED BLACK OUTLINES WHICH ARE DELIBERATELY ONLY LOOSELY REGISTERED TO THE BASIC BODY SHAPES, BUT GIVE AN EXTRA LIVELINESS TO THE LEAPING ANTELOPES AND TROTTING ELEPHANT.

ABOVE AND RIGHT:
THIS PROCION-DYED FABRIC – MADE UP AS A CUSHION COVER OPPOSITE – WAS DYED FIRST.
THE WHITE COCKEREL WAS THEN LINO BLOCK-PRINTED USING OPAQUE WHITE PIGMENT DYESTUFF.
YOU CAN SEE THAT WE LEFT ENOUGH LINO ON THE BLOCK TO PRINT A FAINT WHITE SURROUND
TO THE COCKEREL.
FINALLY, THE COCKEREL WAS OVERPRINTED WITH A BLACK OUTLINE (AGAIN WITH A LINO BLOCK).
THIS APPROACH IS REALLY ANOTHER WAY OF GETTING A RESIST 'FEEL' WITHOUT ACTUALLY USING WAX
OR PASTE RESISTS.

These two photographs illustrate the difference in 'feel' between a wax resist (large photograph) and a screen-printed version of the same motif. Undoubtedly the screen print produces a more positive result but has none of the beauty of the indigo wax resist version, shown here being overprinted with a lino-block black outline.

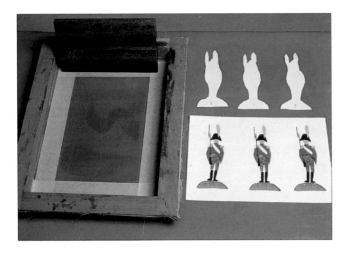

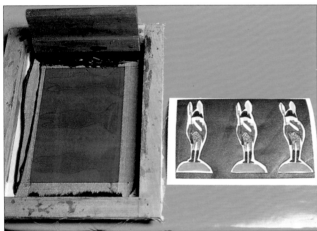

IN ANOTHER EXAMPLE OF MIXED TECHNIQUES, WE POTATO PRINTED OUR PARADE OF BRAVE SOLDIERS, THEN SCREEN PRINTED THE BACKGROUND COLOUR.

TOP LEFT: THE POTATO-PRINTED SOLDIERS ARRANGED AGAINST A PLAIN BACKGROUND. ABOVE THEM YOU CAN SEE THE PAPER STENCILS WE CUT OUT TO PROTECT THEM DURING THE SILK-SCREEN PROCESS. TO THEIR LEFT YOU CAN SEE THE SCREEN READY TO RECEIVE THE SOLDIERS AND STENCILS.
ABOVE: THE BACKGROUND TO BE PRINTED WITH THE SOLID COLOUR AND THE STENCILS IN PLACE COVERING THE SOLDIERS.
LEFT: THE COMPLETE PRINT, SHOWING THE SOLDIERS VIGNETTED AGAINST THE BACKGROUND COLOUR.

WE HAVE CHOSEN OUR ANTELOPE CUSHION TO DEMONSTRATE IN DETAIL HOW COMBINING A SEVERAL
TECHNIQUES CAN PRODUCE VERY EFFECTIVE RESULTS. HERE, THE SOLID YELLOW AREA HAS BEEN
SILKSCREENED AND THE NEGATIVE WHITE SPACES LEFT BY OVERPRINTING STENCILS HAVE THEN BEEN
OUTLINED IN BLACK PRINTED WITH LINO BLOCKS.

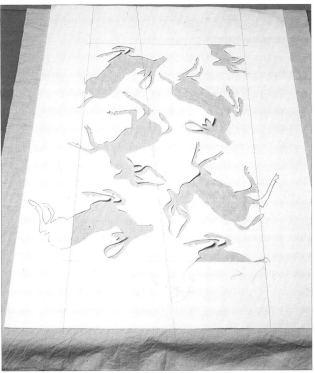

ABOVE LEFT: POSITIVE STENCILS ON THE FABRIC.

ABOVE: NEGATIVE STENCILS ON THE FABRIC.

LEFT: HERE THE SILK SCREEN IS SHOWN RESTING ON THE POSITIVE STENCILS IMMEDIATELY PREPARATORY TO PRINTING.

133

ABOVE: YELLOW PIGMENT DYESTUFF BEING PRINTED
OVER THE POSITIVE STENCILS,
WHICH WILL LEAVE THE ANIMAL SHAPES
REVERSED OUT OF THE COLOUR.

ABOVE RIGHT: PRINTING OVER NEGATIVE STENCILS,
WHICH WILL PRODUCE THE ANIMAL SHAPES
IN SOLID YELLOW.

RIGHT: FABRIC PRINTED WITH POSITIVE AND
NEGATIVE STENCILS.

134

RIGHT AND BELOW RIGHT: THE ANTELOPE SHAPE
HAS BEEN CUT OUT IN OUTLINE ON A LINO BLOCK,
WHICH IS THEN USED TO PRINT A BLACK OUTLINE
ON BOTH POSITIVE AND NEGATIVE PRINTS.

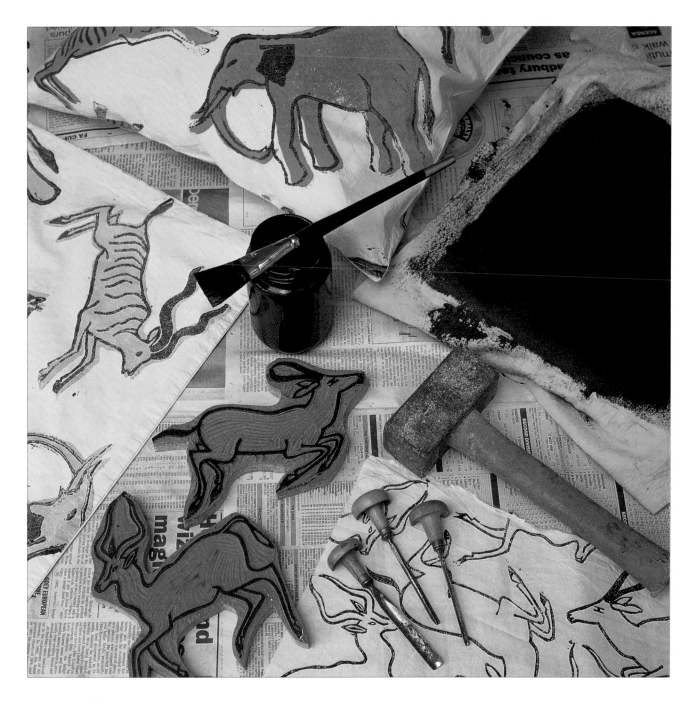

THE TWO BLOCKS SHOWN HERE HAVE BEEN USED TO PRINT THE FABRIC ON THE RIGHT.
AS MUCH OF THE BACKGROUND HAS BEEN CUT AWAY AS POSSIBLE, IN ORDER TO
ACHIEVE AS CLEARLY DEFINED A PRINT AS POSSIBLE. VARIATIONS AND EXPERIMENTAL
PIECES OF CLOTH ARE ALSO SHOWN — OBVIOUSLY, IT IS BEST TO TRY AN IDEA OUT
FIRST BEFORE A LARGE PROJECT IS ATTEMPTED.

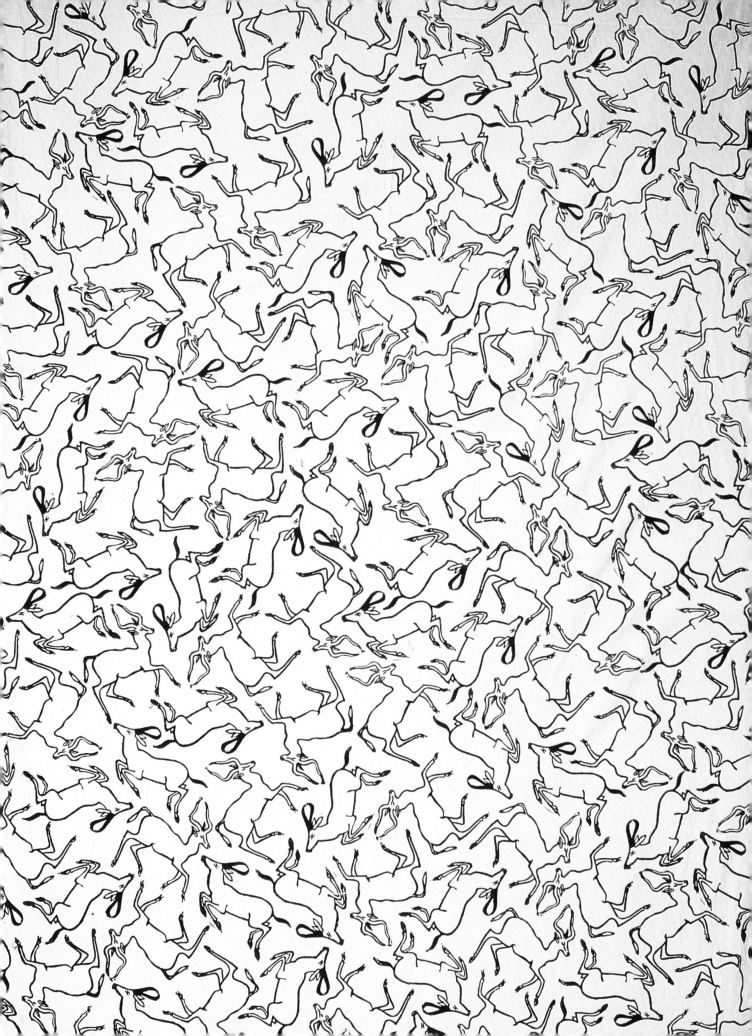

COCKEREL KITCHEN

Our cockerel kitchen evolved from our favourite check tablecloth that we originally printed as a potato print exercise. We enjoyed the bright colouring and decided to extend the idea. We designed the cockerel as a border and after some consideration we decided to potato print all the cloth. This method was ideal anyway for the coloured cockerel but we deliberated whether or not the turquoise checked centre should be printed with a lino block or a silkscreen. We finally decided to use a square cut potato. This way the character of the print would remain the same. Another advantage was that we were able to print it in sections and at different times. We used the trial pieces to make a tea cosy and an egg cosy.

We really needed a change of scale for the cushions and the café curtains so we decided to screen print them. We used five colours and used the same screen for all the colours. We designed the cushions to be 43 cm (18 in) square and drew the cockerel to scale, then we traced the design on layout or tracing paper. We then cut the paper to the exact 43 cm (18 in) square and with the use of carbon paper we built up the design again, using coloured paper this gave us a coloured master copy. From this master copy we traced over the design for each coloured area and laid the tracing over

cartridge paper with carbon paper in between to make stencils, we then cut until we had pieces of paper with all the separate parts of the design. After that we were ready to print as described.

The cockerel was printed in the following order. Yellow body, blue tail, red comb, green border and, in this case, the border was printed four times (one side at a time) as we used a small screen, and finally black feet and beak.

Keep buckets of water to hand and lots of rag and kitchen towel as spots of colour can appear if everything is not squeaky clean.

Do make sure that the screens are absolutely dry before re-using. If you have lots of screens you can use one for each colour. Take care to wash the screen and squeegee very carefully because colour can get trapped. A sunny windy day is ideal for drying the screens – or you can use a hair dryer!

WHEN WE DESIGNED OUR KITCHEN PROJECT WE WANTED TO SHOW A NUMBER OF TECHNIQUES WORKING TOGETHER IN A HARMONIOUS AND NATURAL WAY. THE COCKEREL MOTIF WAS PERFECT FOR POTATO PRINTING AT A SMALL SIZE FOR A DECORATIVE BORDER (ABOVE), BUT NEEDED TO BE SCALED UP AND MADE INTO A SCREEN STENCIL FOR THE CUSHION, CURTAINS AND WALL PRINT SEEN ON THE PREVIOUS PAGE. THE TABLECLOTH WAS PRINTED IN A CHEQUERBOARD PATTERN USING A SQUARE-CUT POTATO. THE BACKGROUND TO THE PICTURE ON THE OPPOSITE PAGE SHOWS THE SQUARES ACTUAL SIZE.

HANDPRINTED FABRICS CREATE A STYLE OF THEIR OWN.
HERE, WITH NOTHING MORE COMPLICATED THAN POTATO PRINTING,
BLUE SQUARES AND JAUNTY COCKERELS COMBINE TO MAKE THE
BRIGHTEST OF SPRINGTIME BREAKFAST TABLES.

CONCLUSION

A great deal of satisfaction and a sense of achievement can be derived by making or doing something yourself. More importantly, perhaps, by being involved in the construction or making of an object, your appreciation of it is enhanced.

Dyeing and patterning, later printing, fabrics and papers are ancient crafts, and like so many crafts much that has been learned and perfected over the centuries has been lost in the last fifty years in the search for more efficient methods of industrialized production. We explained in our Introduction that *Print Style* is not be any means a manual covering all methods and styles of printing. It shows our approach, and we attempt to show what is possible and what can be achieved with minimal space and equipment. We hope it will inspire you not only to experiment with the methods shown, but also to explore and research further.

GLOSSARY

CALICO: Although calico became a general term for cotton woven in India and named after the city of Calicut on the Malabar coast, it more recently simply refers to a plain white or natural cotton fabric.

COLOURWAY: refers to an alternative colouring of a design.

FIXING: describes the process by which dyestuffs, whether printed or dyed, are attached permanently attached to the cloth. Different types of dyestuffs require different treatment and this may involve baking, ironing or steaming the cloth to ensure the finished cloth will be light-fast and colour-fast.

DYESTUFF OR PRINTPASTE: is a combination of dissolved dye, the necessary chemicals and thickening agent (usually a gum) required to print colour onto cloth without the colour spreading.

GUM ARABIC: Water-soluble gum obtained from various species of the acacia plant.

MERCERIZED COTTON: A process invented by John Mercer in

1844 in which cotton, immersed in caustic soda under tension produces a fine silk-like lustre to the surface.

NATURAL FIBRES: are classified under two headings – animal and vegetable. Animal fibres include silk and wool. Vegetable fibres include cotton, linen and jute.

NATURAL OR VEGETABLE DYESTUFFS: Before the discovery in 1856 (by W H Perkin) of the first synthetic dyestuff, mauve, all dye colours originated from natural sources: plants, insects, minerals, even shellfish and lichen – madder, indigo, cochineal and weld are examples.

PIGMENT PRINTING: describes a system of printing used to apply insoluble colour particles held on the surface of a fabric by a binding agent such as albumen or, more recently, oil-in-water type emulsions.

Pigment dyestuffs should not be confused with the use of pigments in other areas of the decorative arts, notably in the manufacture of paints for use on paper, furniture and walls.

– unlike most other classes of dyestuff, pigment dyestuffs can only be used for printing, not dyeing.

– in common with other dyestuffs, pigment printing is recognizable as a class of dyestuffs even though, in common with other dyestuffs, it is available under a variety of trade names. Hence 'Polyprint' or 'Helizarin' refer to the same product type even though there might be some variations in its manufacture.

REACTIVE DYE: A dye such as procion which combines chemically with the fibre on being fixed.

REGISTRATION: refers to the accurate placing of the design on the fabric and where a design consists of more than one colour, ensuring that each colour accurately fits the design.

RESIST: Refers to any substance that can be applied to areas of fabric to prevent the penetration of dye. Ideally, a suitable resist should be easy to apply and remove.

SQUEEGEE: A rubber blade attached to a strip of wood for pushing and pulling dye across the inside of the screen while printing.

SYNTHETIC DYESTUFFS: There are many different types of synthetic dyes and they are usually divided into classes: direct dyes; vat dyes; basic dyes; mordant dyes; acid dyes, and reactive dyes. All have slightly different methods of application or are more suitable for one type of fibre than another. Although the process is different, most synthetic dyes can be used for both printing and dyeing.

VAT DYES: dyestuffs which are insoluble in water, but can be converted to a soluble reduced form when treated with alkaline reducing agent. While in this reduced state, they can be absorbed by textile fibres. On being exposed to the air, oxidation (from oxygen in the air) converts this reduced form to the original insoluble vat dyestuff which is firmly held within the fibre. Indigo is a good example of a vat dye.

WARP: The threads that run lengthwise in the cloth.

WEFT: The threads that run across the cloth.

SOURCES AND SUPPLIERS

EUROPE

POLYPRINT
815 Lisburn Road, Belfast BT9 7GX. Tel (01232) 381410
Pigment dyes for printing fabrics

HAYES CHEMICALS
55 Glengall Road, London SE15 6NF.
Indigo and related chemicals, all types of dyes and dyestuffs

FRANK HERRING & SONS
27 High Street, Dorchester DT1 1UP.
Tel (01305) 267917+264449, Fax (01305) 250675
General art suppliers and textile printing equipment

THE LEYLAND PAINT COMPANY
Huddersfield Road, Birstall, Batley, West Yorkshire WF17 9XA.
Tel (01924) 477201, Fax (01924) 420403. Sales Orders (01924) 42002
Paints

GEORGE WEIL & SONS LTD.
Shop, 18 Hanson Street, London W1P 7DB.
Fabrics and dyestuffs

COURSES:
HINCHCLIFFE AND BARBER
Connegar Farm, Manston, Sturminster
Newton, Dorset DT10 1HB. Tel/Fax (01258) 472644

AUSTRALIA

Art Supplies

ALDAX INDUSTRIES PTY LTD *(Art and craft paints)*
NSW: 64 Violet St, Revesby 2212 Tel (02) 772 1066

ARTISTCARE
NSW: 93 York St, Sydney 2000 Tel (02) 299 4151
VIC: 276–278 Park St, South Melbourne 3205 Tel (03) 699 6188
QLD: 65 Mary St, Brisbane 4000 Tel (07) 210 0566

DEANS ART
NSW: 213 Oxford St, Darlinghurst 2010 Tel (02) 360 2599
VIC: 188 Gertrude St, Fitzroy 3065 Tel (03) 419 6633

Dyes and Dyestuffs

BATIK OETORO
NSW: 203 Avoca St, Randwick 2031 Tel (02) 398 6201

DYE "M" ALL PTY LTD
NSW: 39 Albert St, St Peters 2044 Tel (02) 519 5199

HODGSONS DYE AGENCIES PTY LTD
NSW: 56 Bay St, Broadway 2007 Tel (02) 211 4633
VIC: 11–13 McDonald Lane, Mulgrave 3170 Tel (03) 956 2211
QLD: 3/175 Jackson Rd, Sunnybank 4109 Tel (07) 344 5655
WA: 12 Fargo Way, Welshpool 6106 Tel (09) 356 2688

INDEX

✳

PERTH AND KINROSS LIBRARIES